THE ROLLING STONES
HAVE MADE SOME OF
THE MOST MEMORABLE
MUSIC IN HISTORY
WHILE LIVING OUT A TALE
THAT IS THE VERY ESSENCE OF
ROCK AND ROLL

kp D&C
David and Charles

Foreword

by Valeria Manferto De Fabianis

I WAS A TEENAGER IN THE 60S AND THE SONGS OF THE ROLLING STONES AND THE BEATLES WERE THE SOUNDTRACK TO THAT MEMORABLE PERIOD. WE WERE THE BEAT GENERATION AND WHILE THE ROLLING STONES WERE THE EMBODIMENT OF ANTI- CONFORMISM AND SHOUTED THEIR REBELLION IN THE AUTHENTIC ROCK SPIRIT, THE BEATLES WERE THE STANDARD BEARERS OF RESPECTABILITY WHICH REIGNED ABOVE ALL IN THE OLD CONTINENT. AND WE YOUNG PEOPLE WERE SHARPLY DIVIDED INTO TWO "FACTIONS", AS FANS OF ONE OR THE OTHER.

MY BEDROOM WAS DOMINATED BY A POSTER OF MICK JAGGER WHO GAZED AT ME WITH A SULKY EXPRESSION LIKE AN IRREVERENT AND RATHER ARROGANT BOY. I LOVED THEIR MUSIC AND I LOVED THE ENERGY THAT THEY CONVEYED EVEN MORE, THE SAME ENERGY THAT EVEN TODAY AFTER 50 YEARS AT THE TOP, THEY ARE STILL CAPABLE OF TRANSMITTING WITH THE SAME ARROGANCE AT EVERY CONCERT.

WHEN I WAS WRITING THIS BOOK, GOING OVER THE MILESTONES OF THEIR SUCCESS, I HAD FURTHER CONFIRMATION THAT NOBODY HAS EMBODIED THE SPIRIT OF ROCK BETTER THAN THEM, NOT ONLY IN MUSIC BUT ALSO IN THE WAY THEY CONFRONTED LIFE, A LIFE MADE UP OF EXCESSES, OF FAILURES AND MIRACULOUS COME-BACKS, NEVER SATISFIED OR TIRED OF LIVING AND LIVING IN TIME WITH THE ROCK BEAT.

ON THEIR FACES, LINED WITH DEEP, MAGNIFICENT WRINKLES, YOU CAN READ THE HISTORY OF THAT MUSIC THAT FROM THE SECOND HALF OF THE 20TH CENTURY HAS PROVIDED THE RHYTHM OF OUR YEARS. YOU CAN SEE THAT THE STRENGTH OF THAT INCOMPARABLE ENERGY REMAINS INTACT AND IT MAKES US REALIZE THAT NOBODY MORE THAN THE ROLLING STONES REPRESENTS, OR SHOULD I SAY PERSONIFIES ROCK.

AND, IT IS FOR THIS REASON, THAT I FEEL THAT I OWE THEM MY MOST SINCERE AND HEART-FELT GRATITUDE.

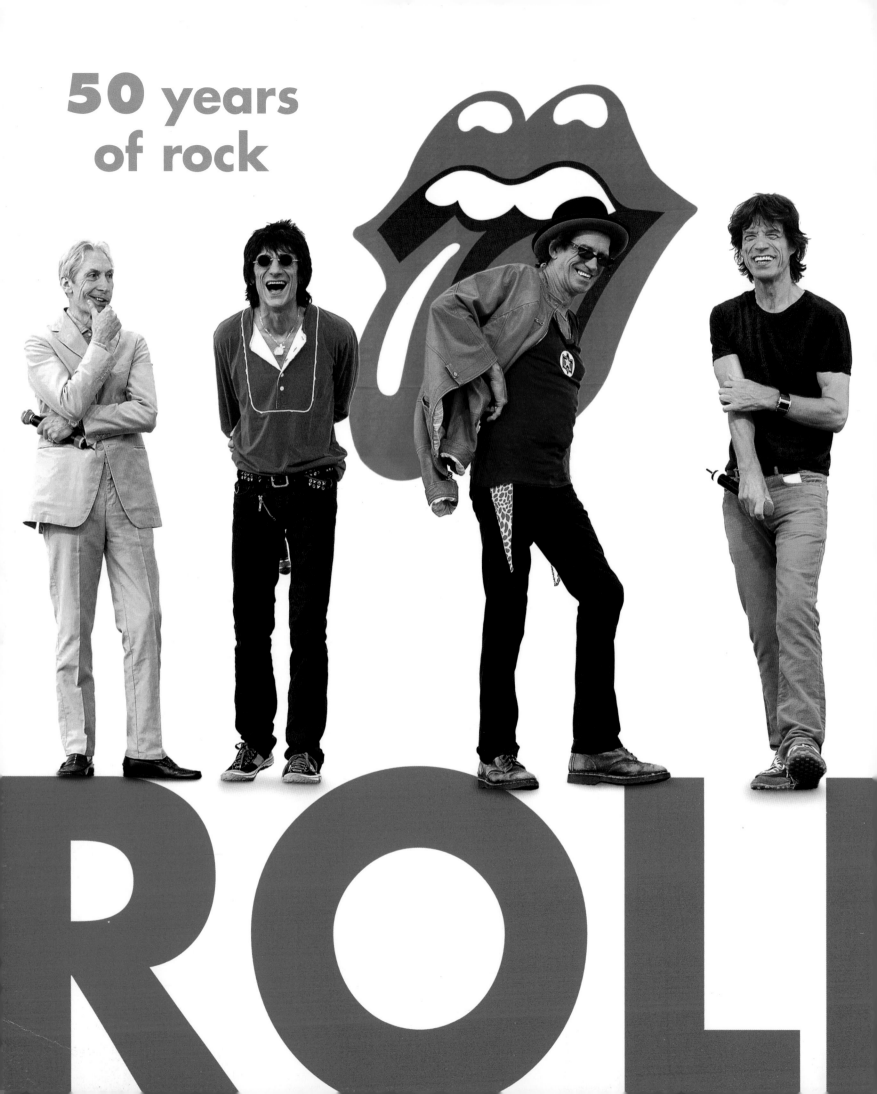

Contents

TEXT BY
HOWARD KRAMER

EDITED BY
VALERIA MANFERTO DE FABIANIS

GRAPHIC DESIGN
MARINELLA DEBERNARDI

ICONOGRAPHIC CONSULTANT
MARCO DE FABIANIS MANFERTO

Introduction

For my wife, Sally, and my children, Sam and Sophie, whose boundless love and endless support enrich my life every day.

THIS IS NOT THE FIRST BOOK ABOUT THE ROLLING STONES. FAR FROM IT. IN FACT, IT'S A SAFE BET TO ASSUME THAT IT WON'T BE ANYWHERE NEAR THE LAST. FOR NEARLY FIFTY YEARS, THE ROLLING STONES HAVE BEEN AN OBJECT OF FASCINATION TO MILLIONS OF FOLLOWERS, CRITICS AND DETRACTORS. FROM THEIR SIMPLE BEGINNINGS AS A SCRUFFY WEST LONDON BLUES BAND THROUGH TODAY, THEIR STORY HAS HELD THE ATTENTION OF MUSIC FANS FROM ALL PARTS OF THE MUSICAL SPECTRUM.

LIKE SO MANY OF THE BRITISH INVASION ERA BANDS, THE ROLLING STONES HELPED BRING THE FIRST GENERATION OF ROCK AND ROLLERS AND THE POST-WAR BLUESMEN TO A WORLD THAT HAD EITHER FORGOTTEN OR IGNORED THEM THE FIRST TIME AROUND. WHEN THE STONES APPEARED ON THE AMERICAN TV SHOW SHINDIG IN 1965, THEY MADE IT A CONDITION OF THEIR APPEARANCE THAT THAT HOWLIN' WOLF ALSO APPEAR. WATCHING THE SHOW NOW, IT'S ALMOST CHARMING TO SEE BRIAN JONES' IMPATIENCE WITH THE HOST'S QUESTIONS AS THEY WAIT TO INTRODUCE THE WOLF'S PERFORMANCE.

CERTAINLY THE STONES PAID RESPECT, BUT THEY ALSO PAID THEIR DUES. THE ONLY WAY TO BE A GOOD BAND WAS TO WORK, AND WORK THEY DID. THE PACE THAT THEY KEPT — SIMILARLY TO THE BEATLES, THE KINKS, THE WHO ETC. — WOULD BE INCONCEIVABLE TO A NEW BAND IN THE 21ST CENTURY. IT WOULD ALSO BE IMPOSSIBLE. THE AVAILABLE VENUES AND MEDIA OUTLETS THAT EXISTED THEN HAVE NO CURRENT PARALLEL. CREATING CONSISTENTLY AT THE LEVEL THEY ACHIEVED, IN THE PRESSURE COOKER IN WHICH THEY EXISTED, MAKES THEIR OUTPUT THAT MUCH MORE IMPRESSIVE. AT SEVERAL POINTS IN THE STONES' STORY, THE MADE MEMORABLE MUSIC AS OTHER FORCES, BOTH INTERNAL AND EXTERNAL, WEIGHED ON THEM.

IN WAYS MORE FAR MORE IMMEDIATE THAN THE BEATLES, THE ROLLING STONES WERE RESPONSIBLE FOR THOUSANDS OF MUSICIANS. THE BEATLES ALMOST SEEMED TOO PERFECT. THEY HAD THE LOOK, THE

SONGS AND NO SMALL AMOUNT OF SHOW BUSINESS ACUMEN. THE STONES POSSESSED AN EDGE THAT, BY CONTRAST, MADE THEIR MUSIC MORE ACCESSIBLE. IT IS NOT AN OVERSTATEMENT TO SAY MUCH OF THE AMERICAN GARAGE ROCK GENRE CAN BE TRACED TO THEM. BEFORE THE MC5 BECAME THE BÊTE'-NOIRE OF THE ESTABLISHMENT, THEY CUT THEIR TEETH OF AS A STONES COVER BAND, PLAYING THE TEEN CLUBS AROUND DETROIT. THIS SORT OF STORY REPEATED ITSELF ALL ACROSS THE WESTERN WORLD.

THE ROLLING STONES HAVE BEEN DECLARED OVER AND DONE ON INNUMERABLE OCCASIONS SINCE THEY FIRST BROKE. EACH TIME, THEY RE-UPPED THE ANTE BY DELIVERING MUSIC THAT HELPED DEFINE THE TIME IN WHICH IT WAS RELEASED AND EVENTUALLY BECAME TIMELESS. DESPITE NO RECENT RECORDS OR PERFORMANCES, THEY REMAIN THE GOLD STANDARD FOR EVERYTHING A ROCK AND ROLL BAND CAN AND SHOULD BE – INNOVATIVE, INSOUCIANT, BALLSY AND TRUE TO THEIR ROOTS. IF AND WHEN THEY CHOOSE TO WORK AGAIN, THE STONES WILL IMMEDIATELY REASSUME THE TITLE THE "WORLD'S GREATEST ROCK AND ROLL BAND." BECAUSE THEY EARNED IT.

2-3 The Rolling Stones in 2005 gathered upon the release of A Bigger Bang.
4 Just a group of English guys who want to play the blues and not wear matching waistcoats.
10-11 In 2006, the Rolling Stones played at the biggest event in American sports, the Super Bowl.
12 "The Human Riff," as Keith Richards has been labeled, is the embodiment of the rock and roll lifestyle fantasy.

13 Mick Jagger is truly the quintessential rock star. He is without equal in his prowess as a showman.
14 Charlie Watts, drummer with the Rolling Stones, looking quizzically over his sunglasses.
15 Ronnie Wood, rock guitarist and bassist, songwriter, producer and artist, member of the Rolling Stones, photographed in the studio on 16th August 1974.

Off the Hook

1962-1968

THE ROLLING STONES
ENGLAND'S NEWEST HIT MAKERS
12 X 5
THE ROLLING STONES NO. 2
THE ROLLING STONES, NOW!
OUT OF OUR HEADS
DECEMBER'S CHILDREN
AFTERMATH
GOT LIVE IF YOU WANT IT!
BIG HITS (HIGH TIDES AND GREEN GRASS)
BETWEEN THE BUTTONS
THEIR SATANIC MAJESTIES REQUEST
BEGGARS BANQUET

There's a mysterious alchemy to how musical groups form. It's an entirely different situation when a central figure surrounds themselves with able-bodied players to help realize a single vision. Actually, bands come together in a manner not too dissimilar from how galaxies form. The gravity of attraction to music, usually music from outside the mainstream, somehow pulls together divergent and seemingly irresolvable elements. These elements evolve over time, sometimes violently, to create an environment where something organic grows and thrives. In this case, it's music. This story has played out an infinite number of times over the course of history to varying degrees of success. What a band is made of – its real measure of how it sustain and thrives – comes down to its work ethic; can you produce under pressure, can you put aside differences enough to keep working, how will you react in the face of extraordinary adversity? The bands who realize that the whole is worth more than the sum of its parts, and work to keep it all together, can sustain and survive. The gestation of the Rolling Stones is a tale of chance. Had Mick Jagger and Keith Richards not been waiting for the same train at the Dartford rail station, had Alexis Korner not created an R&B residency at the Ealing Jazz Club, had Brian Jones not placed an ad in the music papers that resulted in Ian Stewart's response, had Bill Wyman not had a decent amplifier or had Charlie Watts been more wary about job security as a graphic artist, this all may not have happened. But it did. Mostly drawn together by a love of American rhythm and blues music, the Rolling Stones, as we came to know them, made their unheralded debut in January 1963.

The Rolling Stones formed at an incredibly opportune moment in British music history. In 1963, the Beatles rapid rise in stature in the U.K. was leaving some of the old order British teen idol-types in the proverbial dust. Where the Beatles were driven almost exclusively by American rock and roll, the Rolling Stones were driven by American blues and R&B. There was some common ground, most notably Chuck Berry, but there was a more discernable strain of blues purism that informed the Stones. In a world were money didn't matter, that might have been enough to keep the Stones in a Thursday night residency at some pub playing for 80-100 people a week. The Stones were a young, charismatic band who could play convincingly. That set them apart and made them ready for the opportunities that lay before them.

Once they secured a residency at the Crawdaddy Club in Richmond, the Stones quickly began drawing crowds. Within a couple months, they attracted the attention of Andrew Loog Oldham who was, like the band themselves, driven and charismatic. Only 19 years of age, he had already worked PR for the Beatles and knew his way around the British music industry. Oldham signed the band to a management contract and then set his sights on Decca Records A&R man Dick Rowe who had turned down the Beatles. In fact, George Harrison had tipped Rowe to the Stones. Rowe signed the Rolling Stones and within weeks Decca released their debut single.

"Come On" / "I Want to Be Loved" was straight from the well of Chicago-born music that would be the bedrock of the entire career of the Rolling Stones. The a-side was a Chuck Berry composition that he released in 1961 but had not come out in Great Britain. The b-side came was originally recorded by Muddy Waters in 1955 and came from the pen of Willie Dixon, the most prolific blues songwriter and producer. Both were performed at breakneck pace as compared to the originals. The record gives the Stones a foot in the door and peaks at Number 21.

Oldham set about styling the band and his first move was to delegate Ian Stewart to the background. By Oldham's measure, "Stu" didn't fit the profile meriting membership in a successful pop group. To his everlasting credit, Stewart accepted the demotion and stayed with the band as road manager/aide-de-camp/pianist and musical anchor until his death in 1985. Much to the band's chagrin, Oldham made them dress in matching suit jackets and such for their early television performances. It was a situation that didn't sit well or last long.

The Rolling Stones first-ever tour was a six week run covering England, Scotland and Wales. They were billed third, just behind headliners the Everly Brothers and, one of their heroes, Bo Diddley. Midway through the tour, promoter Don Arden brought in Little Richard to shore up sagging ticket sales. For the Stones, the entire trek was nothing short of being thrown into the deep end. It was a truly formative experience for a bunch of, mostly, kids.

Andrew Loog Oldham's connection to the Beatles proved very fortunate for the Stones. The first encounter between the two groups actually came at the instigation of Giorgio Gomelsky, the promoter of the Crawdaddy Club, who invited the Liverpool group to see the band. Oldham knew the Stones needed a new single and, since his group hadn't taken to composing, why not get the hottest composers in Great Britain to provide a song? "I Wanna Be Your Man" by John Lennon and Paul McCartney became the Rolling Stones' second single in November 1963. This record reached Number 12. The b-side, a walking blues quasi-instrumental entitled "Stoned," was credited to Nanker Phelge, a nom-de-plum for the Rolling Stones.

The importance of songwriting is a critical issue to success. Since their beginning, the Rolling Stones have

played other peoples material exclusively. Oldham pressured Jagger and Richards to start creating their own songs. It must have worked because even before the Rolling Stones released a Jagger/Richards composition on one of their own records, British singer George Bean and American singer Gene Pitney did so.

As it was the way things were done, the Rolling Stones worked constantly. Andrew Loog Oldham's business partner, Eric Easton, booked the band all over the U.K. and they played virtually every town in England that had a hall or teen club which permitted pop groups. In between were television appearances and radio sessions. It was the type of pace that tested their mettle and forced them to learn their craft.

1964 kicked off with a run of dates supporting the American vocal group the Ronettes. The Stones and the Ronettes became fast friends and Jagger and Richards dated Ronnie Bennett and her cousin Nedra Talley. An EP was released featuring songs originally performed by Chuck Berry, the Coasters, Barrett Strong and Arthur Alexander. The Alexander composition, "You Better Move On" is a somewhat curious selection. A southern soul singer with a pronounced country inclination, Alexander is barely known in the States, let alone Great Britain. The song is a sweet break-up tale that is well handled by the young Stones.

February had the Stones headlining a four-week long, multi-act bill. While on the road, their third single "Not Fade Away" came out and finally put them near the top of the U.K. charts with a Number Three hit. "Not Fade Away" was a Buddy Holly song that the Stones revved up, taking its Bo Diddley/hambone beat and kicking into overdrive. It also became the Stones first U.S. single. At that moment, the Beatles were exploding all over America. The Stones American label, London Records, had great hopes that the Beatles would have long coat-tails. And though the Beatles did create a breach in America, it was the Dave Clark Five and the duo of Peter and Gordon who were the first to follow successfully. "Not Fade Away" barely made the American Top 50.

By April 1964, the heat was building around the Rolling Stones. The February tour proved they were as much a draw as headliner John Leyton. Perhaps even more telling was the reaction by parents and the media. Partially fueled by Oldham, who knew how to wind up the press, the Rolling Stones were seen as a legitimately menacing counterpart to the Beatles and beginning to generate negative press. Reaction from the establishment didn't seem to dent their growing fan base.

In mid-April, their first long playing album, simply titled the Rolling Stones, hit the streets. Cut over the course of four days in January, it featured 12 cuts, nine of which were American R&B songs. The three exceptions were variously credited to Nanker Phlege, Jagger and Richards, and Phlege/Spector. Gene Pitney and Phil Spector attended the sessions and contributed in various ways. The album is a Number One smash in the U.K. The Rolling Stones also make their international debut with a television performance in Montreux, Switzerland. In America, the album is treated slightly differently as London Records gives the title the prefix England's Newest Hit Makers and drops "Mona" in favor of "Not Fade Away." The album market in the U.S.

is more lucrative at this point in time and all the labels releasing albums by English groups invariably mess with the running order in the name of profitability.

The Rolling Stones arrived in America for the first time on June 1, 1964 and began a brief tour in San Bernadino, California on June 5. On June 10 and 11, the Stones record at Chess Studios in Chicago, the home of so many artists who influenced them. "Tell Me" / "I Just Want to Make Love to You" is a fresh single to coincide with the U.S. tour. It peaks at Number 24. It's also the first single credited to Jagger/Richards. The tour wraps with a concert at the legendary Carnegie Hall in New York on June 20.

At the end of June, the Stones' version of a song written by Bobby Womack and his sister Shirley, "It's All Over Now" was released and it soon became the Stones first U.K. Number One hit single. The U.S. version came out a month later and stalled at Number 26. Next up in America was a version of "Time is On My Side," originally a hit for New Orleans soul singer Irma Thomas. It breaks the Top 10 and reached Number Six.

In September and October, the Rolling Stones headlining tour of the U.K left no doubt that they are in the upper echelon of U.K. groups. Pandemonium broke out at several shows.

The second American album, 12x5, came out in October, just in time for the second American tour. Several of the songs cut in Chicago are included, as well as the past two singles. The Stones appeared on the television program the Ed Sullivan Show, much to the hosts' regret. They also got a spot on T.A.M.I. Show, an ersatz awards program that boasted a line-up of current and future legends: Chuck Berry, the Supremes, James Brown, the Beach Boys, the Miracles and Marvin Gaye among others.

Shortly after they returned home the Rolling Stones scored their second Number One. The song "Little Red Rooster'" was written by Willie Dixon and originally released by Howlin' Wolf in 1961 as a b-side. The notion of a Chicago blues tune being the biggest song in Britain would have been unthinkable a year before. The intensity of the new pool of talent in Britain and the appetite of the public made for a remarkable feat.

1965 began with the release of their second U.K. album, Rolling Stones No.2, a three-week tour of Australia and New Zealand with Roy Orbison, and a performance in Singapore.

With the release of "The Last Time," their sixth U.K single and their ninth overall, the Rolling Stones kicked into full stride creatively. It was their first U.K Number One composed by Jagger and Richards. Based on a slithering guitar hook, a mechanism that they practically came to define, "The Last Time" showed how quickly the Stones had matured as a musical unit. The record began a salvo of hit singles that has few peers in history and cemented their reputation. Between then and May of 1966, the Stones released, in order: "(I Can't Get No) Satisfaction," "Get Off My Cloud," "19th Nervous Breakdown" and "Paint it Black." With each record the Rolling Stones also molded a persona that almost seems fated, in retrospect. Andrew Loog Oldham fueled the idea of the Stones as "bad boys," the yang to the Beatles' relatively clean-cut yin. The lyrics they created rejected the standard love song narrative. Instead, their songs seemed to embrace decadent self-indulgence and chauvinism. Whether the Stones themselves actually subscribed to that point of view is immaterial to the fact that the public ate it up.

The Rolling Stones covered most of the western world that year with two U.K. tours, two U.S. tours and runs in Scandinavia, France, Germany and Austria. A live record, Got Live if You Want It! and a third studio album, Out of Our Heads, were also released. It was also the year that Allen Klein came into the fold. He and Oldham became the group's co-managers. The ramifications of this particular event would be felt throughout their entire career.

Albums still had little meaning as an artistic statement in the U.K. in 1966. Singles still ruled. In the U.S., Bob Dylan had used the format to delineate his growth as an artist. In April 1966 Aftermath was released. It was the first album comprised entirely of Jagger/Richards compositions. For all the comparisons to the Beatles, particularly in the realm of songwriting, Aftermath was one of the last hurdles the Stones had to clear in their pursuit of artistic parity and credibility.

Touring had become difficult on many levels. Like most performers, they band couldn't hear themselves over the din of the crowd. The crowds themselves, particularly in Europe, often became violent and on several occasions, flying bottles or chairs injured members of the Stones. Over the course of the year, the Stones returned to Australia and New Zealand, toured Europe and the U.S. twice and did a three-week U.K run. It would be three years until the Stones returned to the U.S. to perform and seven until they came back to Australia and New Zealand.

During 1965 and 1966 the Rolling Stones had six singles reach the U.K. Top Five with four of them going to Number One. In the U.S., eight of nine singles went to the Top Ten including three Number Ones.

Pressure, both internal and external, began to profoundly affect the group. Their bad boy image became a magnet for law enforcement officials looking to make an example of the band. In February 1967, Keith Richards' home, Redlands, was raided after an anonymous tip. Richards, Jagger and their friend Robert Fraser were all charged with varying drug related charges. The frantic tabloid media in England leapt on the event as fodder to vilify the band. If that wasn't enough cracks in the relationship between the members began to manifest in the wake of a holiday in North Africa taken by Jones, Richards and Jagger. Brian Jones had been involved with German actress and model Anita Pallenberg since 1965. On many occasions, Jones had turned violent and beat up Pallenberg. While in Morocco, a flare up by Jones led to Richards and Pallenberg leaving the country together and Jones behind. Jones was already becoming problematic within the band since the dynamic shifted and Jagger and Richards became the center of the band. With personal relationships now deeply strained, the situation couldn't remain the way it had been. Changes were coming.

With the Beatles mostly silent and no longer touring, the Rolling Stones had an open field before them in early 1967. "Let's Spend the Night Together" did nothing to dispel any notion of the Stones as threat to all public morality. For their appearance on the Ed Sullivan Show, Jagger was persuaded to change the lyrics to "let's spend some time together," rolling his eyes as sang. The b-side, "Ruby Tuesday" was a lovely mid-tempo song with a baroque quality. Each song was a hit in its own right with the a-side going to Number Three in the U.K and the b-side reaching Number One in the U.S. On the heels of the single came the album Between the Buttons. The cover photo sort of summed up where the band was at in that moment; tired, worn and slightly out of focus. It was the last Rolling Stones album produced by Andrew Loog Oldham. With all that happening, the best band in Britain was less than road worthy. The Rolling Stones did only one tour in 1967, a brief European run in March and April.

The trial for the bust at Redlands came at the end of June. Both Jagger and Richards were found guilty and sentenced to jail time. Fortunately for them, their respective stretches in the can were short. Their legal team successfully appealed the sentences with fines and probation were handed down. Just prior, Brian Jones was the target of a raid on his home and he faced the hand of the law for drug charges.

In the middle of all this, the Beatles release their Sgt. Pepper's Lonely Hearts Club Band album, and half a world a way in San Francisco a whole new scene is exploding. The Rolling Stones respond to the new vibe by creating their own brand of psychedelia in the form of Their Satanic Majesties Request. It was their first self-produced album. While it does contain a few good songs, notably "She's a Rainbow," it's not the transition the Stones need musically. The first step in that direction came in early 1968 when they announced that Jimmy Miller, an American best known for his work with the Spencer Davis Group and Traffic, would be producing their next album.

The first session with Miller proved to be a triumph. Just when the band needed to reconnect with the sort of vibrant rock and roll that defined their greatest work to date, they delivered a career-defining classic. Kicking off with an anthemic guitar riff and a menacing open lyric from Jagger, "Jumpin' Jack Flash" is brutally beautiful. Bill Wyman's fat bass lines lay the anchor for Charlie Watts' straight on beat. Keith Richards and Brian Jones weave together a seamless mesh of guitars that soar as the record fades out. Regardless of the record's great chart showing, Number One in the U.K and Number Three in the U.S., the Rolling Stones created a true pillar of rock and roll.

As if they needed to court controversy, "Street Fighting Man" was released as a single in the U.S. in August, just in time for the Democratic Party's national convention in Chicago, which was the scene of clashes between the police and anti-war protesters. Though it was influenced by student riots in Paris, some Americans saw it as a cal to action and the record was banned in many cities.

With their own dissatisfaction with Their Satanic Majesties Request and the maelstrom swirling around them, the Rolling Stones stripped back everything but the basics. It was a headlong immersion into discovering the roots music within themselves. Jagger and Richards rose to the occasion with a slate of stunning compositions that, like Aftermath three years before, proved to be a watershed moment for the band. It was also done with little input from Brian Jones. He had, essentially, checked out without formally leaving. By all accounts he wasn't particularly missed.

The lead track on Beggars Banquet was unlike anything else on the album or that the Stones had previously recorded. "Sympathy For the Devil" was built on a simple piano riff, a muscular bass line and propulsive percussion. Perhaps the single most distinguishing aspect of the song was the very literate and evocative lyrics. The rest of the album was built on acoustic guitars and tasty slide work. Those elements were the basis of almost every track on the album. All told, it is masterwork that more than serves the purpose of righting the ship.

For two and a half days in December the Rolling Stones filmed their first television special. A rock and roll variety show in a tent, the Rolling Stones Rock and Roll Circus features special guests, the Who, Jethro Tull, Taj Mahal and Dirty Mac, a one-off "super group" with Keith Richards, Eric Clapton, John Lennon and Mitch Mitchell. Unsatisfied with their own performance, the Stones shelve the project. It was the final time Brian Jones performed with the Rolling Stones.

16 The Rolling Stones looking cool and casual outside of St. George's Church, Hanover Square, London. The idea of a band like this being in the proximity of a house of worship would soon be considered unthinkable.

21 This photo session proved particularly fruitful as it provided images for three Rolling Stones albums, 12X5 and Out of Our Heads in the U.S. and The Rolling Stones No. 2 in the UK.

26-27 Charlie Watts' case of food poisoning not withstanding, the Stones performed two shows at the Paris Olympia in 1966. Dozens of fans are arrested when a riot breaks out.

ROLLINGSTONES

28-29 Another day, another press call. Was the photographer simply being clever or prescient?

ROLLINGSTONES

30-31 Was it possible that these five young men were the catalysts that would undermine the moral fabric of Britain's youth?

ROLLINGSTONESROLLINGSTONESROLLINGSTONES
ROLLINGSTONESROLLINGSTONESROLLINGS
ROLLINGSTONESROLLINGSTONESROLLINGST
ROLLINGSTONESROLLINGSTONESROLLI
ROLLINGSTONESROLLINGSTONESROLLINGSTONESROLLINGSTONESROLLINGSTO
ROLLINGSTONESROLLINGSTONES
ROLLINGSTONESROLLINGSTONESROL
ROLLINGSTONESROLLINGSTONESROLL
ROLLINGSTONESROLLINGSTONESROLLINGS
ROLLINGSTONESROLLINGSTONESROLLINGSTON
ROLLINGSTONESROLLINGSTONESROLLI
ROLLINGSTONESROLLINGSTONESROLLINGSTON
ROLLINGSTONESROLLINGSTONESROLLINGSTONESROLLINGSTONESROLLINGSTONES

ROLLINGSTONESROLLINGSTONESROLLINGSTONES
STONESROLLINGSTONESROLLINGSTONES
ONESROLLINGSTONESROLLINGSTONES
ROLLINGSTONESROLLINGSTONES
ROLLINGSTONESROLLINGSTONESROLLINGST

ROLLINGSTONESROLLINGSTONESROLLINGSTONES
INGSTONESROLLINGSTONESROLLINGSTONES
ONESROLLINGSTONESROLLINGSTONES
ROLLINGSTONESROLLINGSTONESROLLINGSTONES
NGSTONESROLLINGSTONESROLLINGSTONES
NESROLLINGSTONESROLLINGSTONES
ROLLINGSTONESROLLINGSTONESROLLINGSTONES
LINGSTONESROLLINGSTONESROLLINGSTONES

32-33 Waiting for a train. The Rolling Stones at Victoria Station, London, en route to Brighton for the final performance of their fall 1964 UK tour.

34 and 35 Hurry up and wait; Brian Jones on the set of Ready, Steady, Go!. The Stones performed their newest single "It's All Over Now." It became their first Number One hit. Jones' looks, charisma and musicianship helped establish the Rolling Stones as a legitimate band and not be cast as yet another teen-oriented pop group.

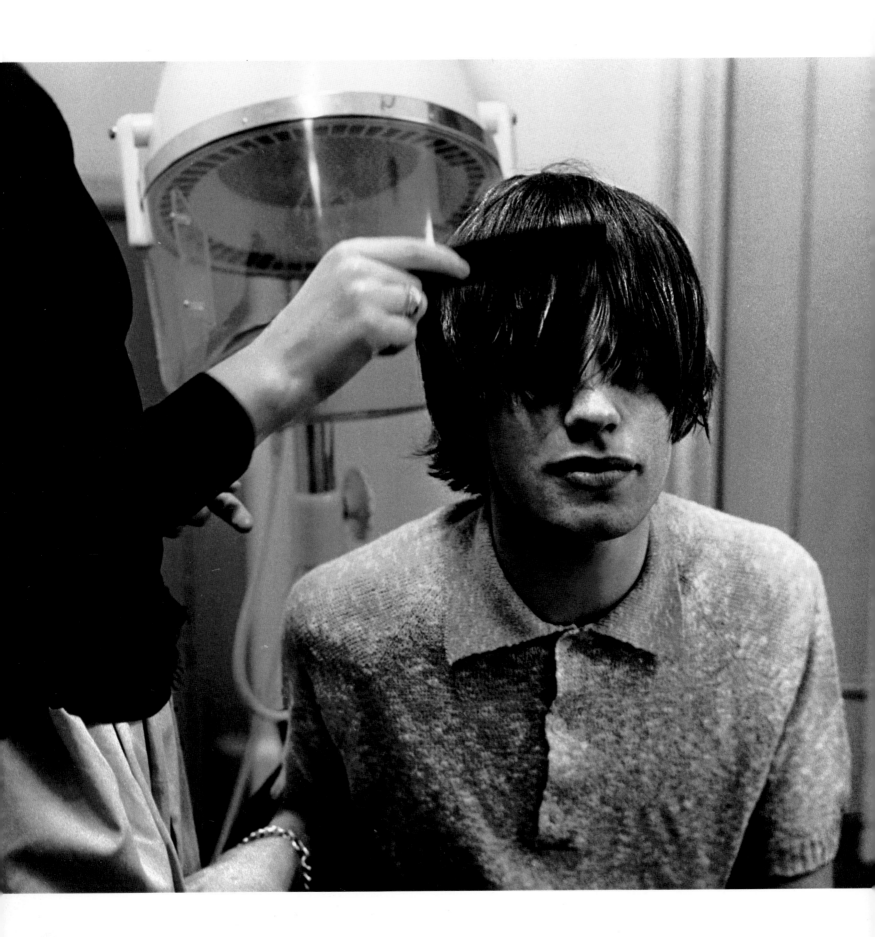

36-37 and 37 What will become of Britain's starving hairdressers? Mick Jagger gets a comb-out in preparation for another television appearance.

38-39 and 39 Eat when you can, sleep when you can. Keith Richards adapts to life on the road and modern furniture design.

40 Keith Richards joyfully succumbs to gravity as he descends from the heights of Montmartre the quick way during a tour stop in Paris.

"WE NEVER WANTED
TO BE POP STARS
WE WERE THINKING
MORE ABOUT JAZZ
OF COURSE
WE REALIZED
THAT WOULDN'T WORK
IF WE WANTED
TO GET INTO
A RECORDING STUDIO"

KEITH RICHARDS

ROLLINGSTONES
ROLLINGSTONES
ROLLINGSTONES

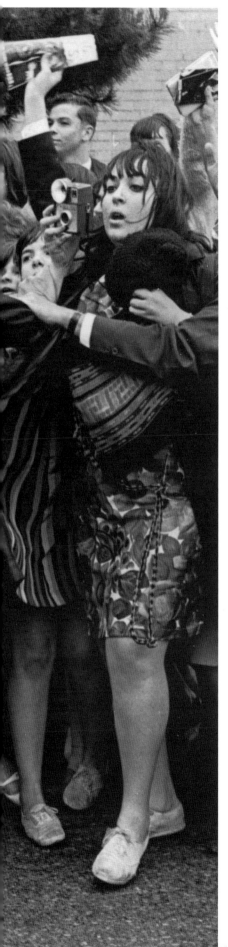

42-43 The Rolling Stones' first U.S. tour was met with varying degrees of indifference except for New York City. Frenzied fans are kept at bay by New York's finest.

43 Anonymity in America was a fleeting luxury for the Rolling Stones. Making a quick getaway from his adoring public is Brian Jones.

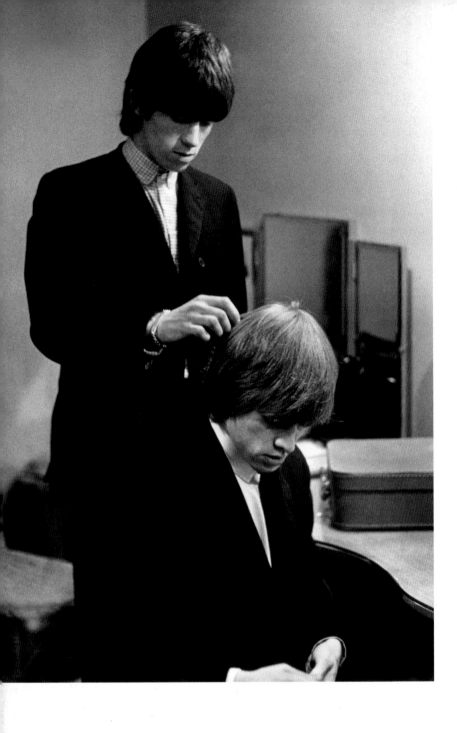

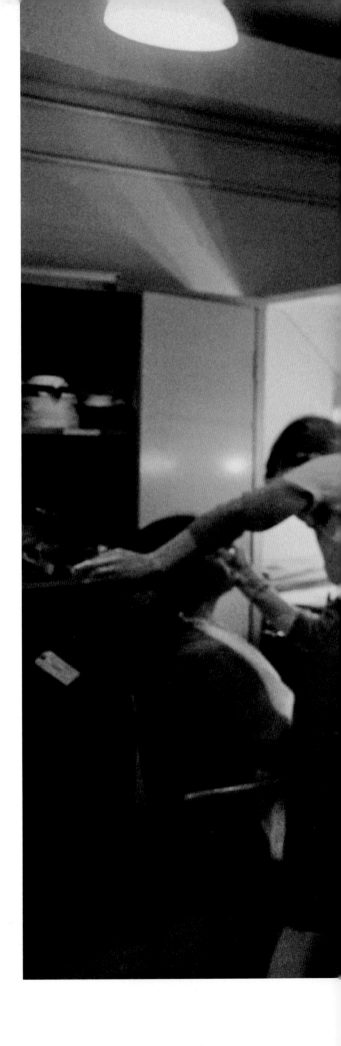

44 In the days before personal stylists, Keith Richards offers some friendly show preparation assistance to his band mate Brian Jones.

44-45 Backstage at Thank Your Lucky Stars, Keith Richards catches a quick shave while his band mates get their make up done.

46 Brian Jones blowing off some steam on the set of Thank Your Lucky Stars in 1964. Jones is playing his teardrop-shaped Vox electric six-string guitar. The Hard Rock Café now owns this instrument.

46-47 Perhaps it's the ludicrousness of miming on television shows that provokes a humorous outburst from Mick Jagger. All bands were required to mime playing their instruments but the vocals only were often live.

48 The Rolling Stones on stage in Copenhagen, Denmark in June 1965. It was their third appearance in the Danish capitol in three months.

49 Fan hysteria mixed with poor security measures and knee-jerk reactions from local authorities often made Rolling Stones concerts spectacles instead of performances.

50 Mick Jagger on Top of the Pops in 1965. By this point, Jagger's skills as a performer made him the most dynamic front man in British rock and roll.

"WHY WOULD YOU WANT TO BE ANYTHING ELSE IF YOU'RE MICK JAGGER?"

KEITH RICHARDS

52 and 53 The scarcity of rock and pop music on the television and radio ma-de each appearance by the Rolling Stones a true event. Shows like Top of the Pops and Thank Your Lucky Stars routinely attracted audiences that rep-resented nearly 20% of the national population.

54-55 With Swinging London in full swing, the Rolling Stones attend another photo call in full contemporary kit.

56 and 56-57 On June 29, 1967, Keith Richard and Mick Jagger stand trail separately for drug related charges. Both are found guilty and sentenced. Appeals are granted the following day. The manner with which the government has unfairly targeted the two musicians is addressed in a scathing editorial in the Times.

58-59 Menacing or exhausted, the Rolling Stones in a 1968 photo session. Tension between the band and Brian Jones were escalating. Jones didn't help matters much with his erratic behavior.

60 and 61 The Rolling Stones in the studio in 1967. By this point in their career, touring had become more trouble than it was worth. Between fan riots, excessive scrutiny from the authorities and an inability to hear themselves, the Stones stayed off the road for more tham two years.

ROLLINGSTONES

62-63 In December 1968, the Rolling Stones filmed their first television special. The Rolling Stones Rock and Roll Circus was shelved and not released until 1996. Seen here joining the Stones at InterTel Studios in Wembley are John Lennon and Yoko Ono at left and Eric Clapton at right.

64-65 The launch party for Beggar's Banquet at the Gore Hotel in Kensington deteriorated into a full-scale pie-throwing melee sparing virtually none of the attendees.

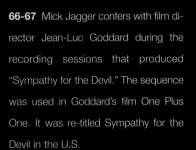

66-67 Mick Jagger confers with film director Jean-Luc Goddard during the recording sessions that produced "Sympathy for the Devil." The sequence was used in Goddard's film One Plus One. It was re-titled Sympathy for the Devil in the U.S.

68 and 69 Jean-Luc Goddard shot the Rolling Stones over the course of two days at Olympic Studios in Barnes as they recorded "Sympathy for the Devil." Lyrically, it was a major milestone in his development as a composer and lyricist.

1962-1968 OFF THE HOOK 1962-1968 OFF THE HOOK 1962-1968 OFF THE HOOK

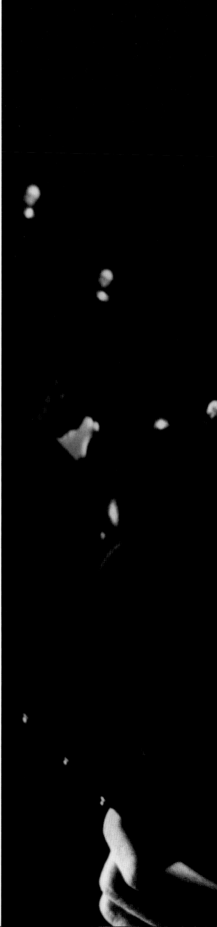

70 and 70-71 Brian Jones had the remarkable talent of being able to play almost any instrument he picked up. In addition to guitar, Jones contributed sitar, saxophone, dulcimer, accordion and oboe to various Rolling Stones recordings. He also guested on recordings by the Beatles and Jimi Hendrix.

1969-1974
You Got the Silver

GET YER YA-YA'S OUT!
LET IT BLEED
THROUGH THE PAST, DARKLY
HOT ROCKS
STICKY FINGERS
EXILE ON MAIN STREET
MORE HOT ROCKS
GOATS HEAD SOUP
IT'S ONLY ROCK N' ROLL

If transition tempered with commercial highs and personal lows defined 1968 for the Rolling Stones, 1969 would be the most tempestuous year of their brief existence. Beggars Banquet was riding high and the Stones were in there traditional chart-position dance with The Beatles' eponymously titled double Lp. Little activity marked the first five months but the remaining seven were disproportionately busy. The band returned to the Olympic Studios in May to cut a song written by Jagger and Richards on their recent South American holiday. "Honky Tonk Women" was a stylistic throwback compared to the rock-cum politics of their last single, "Street Fighting Man." Rootsy, riff-heavy and full of American cultural references, it was written with surprising insight for non-natives. "Honky Tonk Women" was a shot of country soul not too dissimilar to the songs of Arthur Alexander, perhaps the master of blending country and soul.

The session also marked the introduction of guitarist Mick Taylor to the line-up. Whether Brian Jones cast himself out, or he was cast off by the band isn't as important as the fact that the band saw themselves put in a position change or else. Taylor, recently of John Mayall's band, was without a gig but came to the Stones via a conversation between Jagger and Mayall. Although he was only 19, Taylor possessed a keen understanding of the blues. He had stepped into the lead guitar slot in Mayall's band following Peter Green who, in turn had replaced Eric Clapton, perhaps the two best pure blues guitarists Great Britain had produced. Taylor was not privy to the band's plans but a new full length record and a return to touring were already on the slate.

In the early days of June 1969, Jagger, Richards and Watts journeyed to Jones' recently purchased home at Cotchford Farm, where A.A. Milne had written Winnie the Pooh. There they told Jones he was out of the band. The funeral-like atmosphere of the meeting was difficult on all the participants but the tone was civil and all left on good terms and a plan in place to announce the change. The June 14 edition of Melody Maker tells of Jones' departure, Taylor's new gig and a planned return concert at the Coliseum in Rome in less than two weeks, which does not take place. A free show at Hyde Park on July 5 is also announced. The Stones begin to rehearse their new guitarist and prepare to re-enter the studio.

On July 3, Brian Jones dies at age 27. He was found in the swimming pool of his home. The post mortem, conducted by Dr. Albert Sachs of the Royal Victoria Hospital, East Grinstead, West Sussex, portrays Jones in poor physical condition at his time of death. His heart and liver are enlarged and his urine contains 1200 micrograms of amphetamines. The cause of death is officially listed as "death by misadventure." Jones' death also serves to portend the tragedies that will befall Janis Joplin, Jimi Hendrix and Jim Morrison in the ensuing years.

The Hyde Park show is the Rolling Stones first full-length UK show in three years. It's partially repurposed from a return to form into a mass memorial attended by nearly 300,000. Jagger reads a poem by Shelley and butterflies are released. Film of the show reveal a band on a knife-edge from the weight of events and possessing the courage and will to overcome all adversity. Oddly, the full-length film remains unreleased until 2007.

"Honky Tonk Women," the final Rolling Stones single of the decade, rolled out in July and quickly becomes Number One in both the U.S. and the U.K. Its B-side, "You Can't Always Get What You Want," recorded the preceding year, is a sprawling epic and a daring experiment. Starting with a gentle folk riff and a reflective story line, it veers into lush orchestration and a soaring choir that pulses with a gospel stomp, courtesy of drummer/producer Jimmy Miller.

By this point in the summer of 1969, the Rolling Stones had cut much of their next album in several sessions at Olympic Studios. So fruitful were the sessions that tracks from them would continue to appear on new Stones releases for many years to come. A break of sorts was taken as Mick Jagger decamped to Australia to film his dramatic debut as the title character in the film biography of Ned Kelly. Keith Richards and Anita Pallenberg welcomed the birth of a son, Marlin. In America, meanwhile, more than half a million people gather at dairy farm in upstate New York for what is billed as an Aquarian Fair. The Woodstock Music and Art Festival became an event that tipped all perceptions about the weight and meaning of popular and contemporary culture. The Isle of Wight concert, highlighted by the return of Bob Dylan, did much the same. The ideals espoused and practiced at both events would be challenged in short time.

In September, Decca Records released Through the Past Darkly, the second Rolling Stones greatest hits package in September 1969. Featuring a distinctive octagonal package, the set is intended as a tribute to Brian Jones, gloomy title not withstanding.

With the entire band now stationed in Los Angeles, the Rolling Stones get back to work. There is an album to complete and tour to be done. The Rolling Stones sixth North American tour features them performing 22 shows in 15 cities. It will be their first tour of the U.S. in three years and the first tour of any sort since 1967. The brief uproar over ticket prices is rendered moot by the fact that the shows sell-out instantly. Although the Beatles were still the most important rock band, their unwillingness to tour left a huge vacuum. The Stones not only filled it, they burnished their reputation as "the greatest rock and roll band in the world" by hitting the boards and proving it night after night. They faced the scale of these new ventures by inventing the template for arena scaled concerts. The music business would never be the same and the touring industry was born.

By any measure, the tour was an artistic triumph. The entire band was re-energized by the presence and musical prowess of Mick Taylor. Augmenting the band on stage was Nicky Hopkins on keys, Jim Price on trumpet and Bobby Keys on sax. Ian Stewart, as always, played on what he deemed worthy. With all there elements in place, the Stones had the platform to dig their claws even deeper in all the forms of American music that had always fascinated them, Southern-style soul in particular. During the tour, a week-long break found the Rolling Stones in Muscle Shoals, Alabama to record. Seeking to drink at the well that had produced so many wonderful records – "Mustang Sally" by Wilson Pickett, "You Better Move On" by Arthur Alexander (recorded by the Stones in 1963), and "Tell Mama" by Etta James – they cut three songs that would show up on their next studio album.

As all had gone remarkably well at Hyde Park, the Stones sought to repeat the idea and stage a free concert in San Francisco's Golden Gate Park as a tour finale. The city was not so keen on the idea and refused to issue the necessary permits. Altamont Speedway, an auto race track some 50 miles due east of San Francisco, becomes the last minute location. The event is a mess. Nearly 500,000 pour into a site that is ill-prepared for an event of such scale. The staging is low, the toilets and food facilities are few and security is attended to by the Hell's Angels motorcycle club. The extraordinary line-up of bands is each challenged by the experience. Santana cuts their set short. Jefferson Airplane singer Marty Balin is punched out by a Hell's Angel and the band is all but run off the stage. The Flying Burrito Brothers set is uneventful but Crosby, Still, Nash and Young have to deal with more chaos. The Grateful Dead are supposed to play the penultimate set but defer to the Stones in hopes of diffusing the tension that plagues the concert. By the second song of the Rolling Stones' set, the events of the day seem to culminate in a flurry of violence. Jagger's exhortations to the crowd and all around the stage appear to be unheard. Though the band continues to play, tragedy unfolds before them as concertgoer Meredith Hunter is fatally wounded just steps in front of the stage. Oblivious to this, the Stones finish their set and are forced to make hasty retreat and leave the grounds by helicopter. The show is done and the Dead do not play a note. Altamont became a symbol of the antithesis of everything that youth counter-culture had hoped to achieve despite all efforts.

Back in London, the Rolling Stones ended the year with Christmas shows at the Saville Theatre and the Lyceum Ballroom. Reporting on the event for Melody Maker, Chris Welch filed a report of half-hearted praise. He quotes Jagger saying "The most blasé audiences in the world are in our own country, which is why we don't play here." Let it Bleed, released a few weeks before, was riding high in both the U.S. and U.K. charts. It was the first Rolling Stones album from which no singles were culled. From tragedy to triumph, and back again.

No matter how much progress the Rolling Stones made, there always seemed to be an endless series of obstacles before them. While some were self-made, others were well beyond their control. The law enforcement community of England seemed to have included arresting and prosecuting members of the Rolling Stones in their prime directive. Business decisions from the earliest part of their career through to the most recent efforts to amend them had gone awry. As the shadow cast by the Beatles was about to dissipate, the Who and Led Zeppelin were in ascension as recording artists and performers giving the Stones more friendly rivalries to stoke their competitive spirit.

As 1970 opened the group was, fundamentally, without a manager. Their relationship with Allen Klein was rapidly deteriorating. That did not stop them from forging ahead. The first part of the year had Ian Stewart and production director and designer Chip Monck traversing Europe to scout locations for a major tour. Glyn Johns reviewed and began mixing tapes for a live record. The band resumed cutting tracks at Olympic and also put their new mobile recording studio to work. Custom built within the back of an enclosed truck, the Rolling Stones Mobile Unit allowed the group to record almost anywhere and anytime. Jagger's new home, Stargroves was the first locale for remote recording and the first half of the year yielded a new trove of recordings that well followed the sessions in Los Angeles and Muscle Shoals.

Around the same time, a surreptitious recording of one of the Oakland, California shows, entitled Liver Than You'll Ever Be, became the first full-length Rolling Stones bootleg album. London Records quickly went to court in an effort to squelch it. In the era prior to internet file-sharing and easy downloads, concert recordings, old BBC broadcasts and studio outtakes from the Rolling Stones were made into some of the most desirable non-authorized recordings to come to market.

In June, Ned Kelly, starring Mick Jagger, had its world premier in London. After a pallid response from the press, Jagger put some distance between himself and the project by diminishing the entire film.

The end of July 1970 saw a fit of activity that would change many things in the world of the Rolling Stones. The Rolling Stones officially informed Allen Klein that neither he nor ABKCO possessed any rights to represent or negotiate on the band's behalf. The relationship with Klein was, in fact not all over, it would only change in nature. The contract with Decca Records terminated and the band informed the label that they would not be re-signing with them. Their contractual obligation would be fulfilled with the delivery of the new live record.

In late August, the five-week long European tour finally gets under way. For their first continental trek in three years, the Rolling Stones brought large-scale touring to Europe. The groundwork laid by Stewart and Monck the previous months resulted in a production that necessitated a crew of 26 and a touring party of 51. Aside from what Bill Wyman casually referred to as "the odd riot," the shows are ecstatically received. Facing devoted fans in Finland, Sweden, Denmark, the Netherlands, West Germany, France and Italy the Stones again proved their place in the pantheon of English rock bands. Even with playing to larger crowds, the economics of the tour resulted in a net loss. Mick Taylor's role as primary lead guitarist allows Richards to anchor himself in the riffs that he has begun to explore on a seemingly sub-atomic level. Listening to Get Your Ya-Ya's Out, the live album captured at shows in Baltimore and New York and released just as the European tour closes, illustrates the tightness of the band. The spatial mix puts the listener directly in front of the stage with each instrument approximating its location on the stage. Compared to Got Live if You Want It, Ya-Ya's is a sign of maturity. Gone are the screaming teeny-boppers and short sets. The pacing, songwriting, fidelity and musicianship are nothing short of brilliant.

As the year comes to an end, David and Albert Maysle's documentary of the 1969 tour has its cinematic debut. Not a simple visual accomplice to Ya-Ya's, Gimme Shelter is a candid portrait of the band on and off stage. The concert footage, mostly from the Madison Square Garden shows, also includes harrowing footage from Altamont. The film serves as the measuring stick for virtually every concert film that follows.

The premise of the music business has always seemed to be that the artist, be it performer or songwriter, existed only to generate money which would be reaped by the publisher, the promoter, the record company, manager, agent or any other number of often parasitic shysters. If there were some scraps left for the artist, they were supposed to be grateful they got that much. In the rock and roll era, that didn't change all that much. There were a few notable exceptions. Colonel Tom Parker created a system that funneled significant portions of money from everything Elvis Presley was a part of directly to Elvis. The trade off, of course, was artistic atrophy. Fats Domino and Dave Bartholomew retained control of their remarkable publishing catalog. None of their contemporaries could make the same claim. Rock and roll may have affected change to the social order by the mid-Sixties, but the old guard in the music business still ruled. Perhaps the Beatles, with their unprecedented success, could have exerted enough leverage to change things to their favor and, in turn made it better for artists. But they didn't. In 1971, the Rolling Stones found themselves in a horrible dilemma. They learned that Allen Klein now owned their master recordings and the publishing rights to everything dating back to 1962. Additionally, because of the income they generated, the individual band members were subject to U.K. income taxes rates approaching 90%. The Rolling Stones were left with little choice but to relocate to France as tax exiles. It would give them the opportunity to get their financial house in order. They were broke, but not broken.

The idea of forming their own record label had been a key component of the Rolling Stones' business strategy. As true free agents, they had their pick of any and all suitors. They decided to sign with Atlantic Records. It wasn't because Atlantic had made the most lucrative offer. The key factor was that Atlantic was headed by Ahmet Ertegun. The son of Turkish diplomat, Ertegun founded Atlantic in 1947 with Herb Abramson, who left the company in the early Fifties. Jerry Wexler left Billboard Magazine to join the company, which he and Ertegun then built into the premier R&B label. Among the talent they fostered were Ray Charles, Big Joe Turner, LaVern Baker, Ruth Brown, the Clovers, the Drifters, and Clyde McPhatter and many others. In 1971 Atlantic was part of a larger corporate entity, funded by a parking lot empire, but Ertegun still ruled his fiefdom. According to Ertegun, the deal was solidified when he fell asleep sitting at a table with Jagger at the Whisky a-Go Go in Los Angeles. Jagger was impressed by Ertegun's lack of a hard sell. It was, in fact, the result of a night spent drinking.

On March 4, the Rolling Stones began a nine-city tour that the press billed as a farewell tour, in light of the breaking news of the group's impending relocation to France. Anticipation was high as the Stones had not toured Great Britain in five years. During the sold-out tour, the band is firing on all cylinders seemingly unaffected by near constant maelstrom surrounding them. A bootleg of the March 13 show at Leeds University (the same venue where the Who recorded their seminal live record a year before) revels the band to be far from nostalgic as they eschew virtually any originals recorded before 1968, save for "Satisfaction." Shortly after the tour wraps, they film a performance at London's Marquee club with the intension of broadcasting it later that year. Ironically, all three major U.K. television broadcasters pass on the project. It is, however, screened in several European countries,

"Brown Sugar"/"Bitch" is the first record released on the new Rolling Stones Records label, arriving April 16. It was the first new single from the band in nearly two years, not that they hadn't been working. The a-side is a Mick Jagger composition originally cut in Muscle Shoals 18 months before. The b-side hails from Keith Richards' deep mine of riffs. Both songs are sharp tributes to American R&B, complete with punchy horns and hard driving riffs. It's a massive hit on both sides of the Atlantic reaching Number One in the U.S and Number Two in the U.K. A week later, the full length album Sticky Fingers is released. The cover art, designed by Andy Warhol is a photograph of a man in jeans and features a working zipper. In Spain, the artwork is considered obscene and is replaced in that country only by a ghastly photo of severed fingers suspended in bloody treacle. The Rolling Stones Records logo debuts and is a two-color lips and tongue cartoon, clearly patterned after Jagger, and designed by John Pasche. The original artwork now resides in the permanent collection of the Victoria and Albert Museum in London. Sticky Fingers is yet another chart topper around the world. Two hit compilations, one put out by Decca in the UK and London in the U.S are released over the objections of the band.

The group decamps en masse to the south of France to take up residence. Keith Richards' house at Ville Nellcôte becomes the locus of activity. With the Rolling Stones "Mighty Mobile" truck parked at the house and no further touring planned for the year, they begin to jam and write. Nellcôte is an extension of Richards' personality; loose and funky. Band, crew, friends, family and no shortage of hangers-on move through the house at all hours. Conversely, this same atmosphere permits the proliferation of hard drugs to become a problem for some of the band and Richards in particular. Nonetheless, the atmosphere for creativity is rich. Gram Parsons, formerly of the Byrds and then with the Flying Burrito Brothers, is a regular habitué and his presence around the band, and Keith in particular. Parsons' keen interest in country music has rubbed off on Richards and the results are heard in "Dead Flowers" and "Wild Horses," which Parsons recorded and released the previous year with the Flying Burrito Brothers. This vibe is part of the spectrum American roots music the Rolling Stones delve into.

During the course of their stay in France, Mick Jagger married Nicaraguan-born Bianca Perez Morena de Macias in St. Tropez in May. Their daughter, Jade, was born the following October. In August, two separate court actions by the Rolling Stones seek to recover money from Andrew Loog-Oldham and Eric Easton, and Allen Klein, respectively.

Old personality conflicts lead to childish behavior and the sessions in France eventually bog down. In an attempt to get things in motion, the band relocates the operation to Los Angeles to wrap the album and the year.

As 1972 begins, the Rolling Stones continue working in Los Angeles on their latest record. Their legal troubles with Allen Klein eventually reach a working settlement and Klein's ABKCO begins to assist the Stones in their still-pending suit with Andrew Loog-Oldham and Eric Easton over royalties. The second full-length release from Rolling Stones Records, a hold-over from the Let it Bleed session entitled Jammin' With Edward, hits the shelves. Cut during a session that Keith Richards chose to boycott, the record features Mick Jagger, Charlie Watts, Bill Wyman, Nicky Hopkins and noted American guitarist Ry Cooder. This record alone may be responsible for Cooder's well-known distaste for Englishmen.

Heroin had dug deeply into the Rolling Stones. According Wyman, it wasn't just Richards who had a habit, but he was certainly emblematic of the problem. With a full docket of business obligations to fulfill, the need to clean up became apparent. In March, Richards entered a clinic in Switzerland to dry out and get clean.

"Tumbling Dice" / "Sweet Black Angel" is released in mid-April. The "Tumbling Dice" is built around a mid-tempo chugging riff, a laid-back beat and a soulful delivery by Jagger. Lyrically, the song is a more sophisticated take on the traditional blues theme of the backroom gambler whose fortune in craps is a metaphor for his luck in love. The song's unique feature of a drop-off just prior to the chorus eliminates the traditional middle-eight of a pop song and provides the basis for a break-down and build up for the long fade out. 'Sweet Black Angel" is a swampy, percussion-laden song that sounds like a cross between a Lead Belly fable and an ancient traditional tune from some Caribbean island. The single is a Top 10 hit in the U.K and the U.S.

The following month Exile on Main Street arrived. It is the first double album by the Stones and it is met with some skepticism. Writing for Rolling Stone Magazine, Lenny Kaye states the band "take a minimum of chances" and has created a work that is "their most dense and impenetrable." Kaye assessment isn't altogether incorrect. The sonic density of the record is in opposition to the cleanliness of most radio-ready records from major rock acts. The Beatles only double album was met with the same sort of reaction. The major difference being that the Beatles went horizontal in search of sounds and the Stones dived head-first in the well.

Blues and boogie abound throughout Exile on Main Street. Slim Harpo's "Shake Your Hips" and "Casino Boogie" are deep Chicago-via-Memphis nightclub blues tunes held down by mesmerizing piano work from Nicky Hopkins and Ian Stewart. "Turd on the Run" is a frenzied Mississippi hoedown that could have burned down a juke-joint in the hands of Sonny Boy Williamson. The feeling of Southern-style soul gospel is a recurring sound as heard in "Shine a Light," "I Just Want to See His Face" and "Soul Survivor." Even with such full-on rock and roll tracks like "Happy," "Rocks Off," and "All Down the Line" there is no obvious concession to anything. The album becomes a Number One hit on both sides of the Atlantic. What time has shown is that Exile on Main Street is the bookend to the run of studio albums that began with Beggars Banquet in 1968.

The Rolling Stones seventh tour of North America is announced and the band returned to Los Angeles for rehearsals. It runs from June 3 in Vancouver and ends in New York City on July 26, on Jagger's 26th birthday. There are a total of 50 shows in 31 cities with venues ranging from the intimate Hollywood Palladium to the Rubber Bowl, an outdoor stadium in Akron, Ohio. It is an immediate sellout. The band has adapted well to the large venues by bringing state-of-the-art stage production to new levels. Jagger has forged a new look in his stage appearance in the form of slinky jumpsuits made for him by English designer Ossie Clark.

The filmmaker Robert Frank is along with the band for the entire tour and two distinct motion pictures are the result. Concerts in Fort Worth, Texas and Philadelphia, Pennsylvania were shot with the intension of creating a concert film. Directed by Rollin Binzer, the film is a choppy affair that seems to miss the real qualities of the Rolling Stones in concert. Frank's behind the scenes footage is an account of the decadence, mischief and boredom that permeate any tour. Taking the name of an unreleased Stones song, Cocksucker Blues is deemed to cast the band in an unfavorable light and is effectively shelved for decades. All told the Rolling Stones 1972 tour is the most successful outing by any band in history and grosses $4 million.

There would be no rest for anybody as their commitment to Atlantic required them to deliver another studio album for the next year. Tours of Japan, Australia, New Zealand and a return to Europe are also in the works. Pressing legal matters still loomed. Authorities in France were looking into allegations that the Rolling Stones had trafficked in drugs during their stay there. They couldn't go back to England lest they face the tax man so, after some sessions in Jamaica, the entire band, minus Keith went back to France to speak with the authorities. Fortunately for the Jagger, Watts, Wyman and Taylor, the allegations were withdrawn and the investigation closed. Arrest warrants were issued by the French for Richards and Anita Pallenberg, preventing them from setting foot in France. This whole affair, coupled with past run-ins with the law, would impact the forthcoming tour. The Japanese refuse to grant visas to the Rolling Stones. Australia was also reticent to allow the band in.

As this cloud of gloom hung over the band, news arrived of a catastrophic earthquake in Nicaragua, Bianca Jagger's home country. The Jaggers left Jamaica, where the band had resumed recording, and went to Managua, the capital, to search for Bianca's family. They found them unharmed.

The Rolling Stones announce they will play a benefit for the survivors of the Nicaraguan earthquake on January 18, 1973 at the Forum in Los Angeles. Joining them on the bill are Tower of Power, Santana, comedy duo Cheech and Chong and Billy Preston. Over $500,000 is raised and it exceeds the Concert for Bangladesh as the highest grossing charity concert in history. The Australians agree to let the Stones return but Japanese officials stand firm and deny entry. Dates in Hong Kong are also added and then cancelled. The result is a shortened tour and a financial loss. It would be nearly two decades until the returned to these locales. The whole affair kicked off in Hawaii, their first shows there since the 1966 U.S. tour closer.

The band members cannot reestablish residency in England due to the nagging issue of income taxes and are living in multiple locations around the globe. This creates an interesting turn for the band as they are branded with the image of being jet-setters, peripatetic musical gypsies who live the rarefied life of decadent rock stars. Whether any grains of truth apply to this moniker, it does burnish their image as the alpha rock band in the world. Upon delivery of their new album to Atlantic, another dispute arises. Ahmet Ertegun is furious about the track "Starfucker." The subject matter, groupies, the language and the title are a potential powder keg. After some negotiations the band concedes and changes the name to the innocuous "Star Star." Jagger even does a re-dubbed vocal.

The single, "Angie" / "Silver Train" is released in August. A full-on acoustic ballad sung with a bit of Jagger's country twang, "Angie," is unlike anything the Stones have released as a single since "As Tears Go By." The inspiration of the song is variously rumored to be David Bowie's wife Angela and / or Bianca Jagger. No matter the source, the song is another massive hit, securing the Stones their first Number One in the U.S. since "Brown Sugar" two years earlier. "Angie" peaks at Number Five in the U.K. "Silver Train," which Texas blues guitar wizard Johnny Winter released a version of shortly before this, is another Chess-influenced rocker straight from the Rolling Stones comfort zone.

With the release of Goats Head Soup, the Stones had turned a page. There's a more contemporary feel to this than any other full length record since Their Satanic Majesties Request. And while that album from 1967 was not too dissimilar from numerous other artists who walked on the Sgt. Pepper footpath, Goats Head Soup was more an organic product of its times and the times of the band. They hadn't, however, shed their blues roots despite accusations. "Dancing with Mr. D" is built around a simple guitar riff which gives room for Charlie Watts to insert a Philadelphia-style dance beat. Sounds of funky clavinet and Motown-influenced song structures showed how well the band had mastered their craft. Many of the songs sounded as if they were taken from the Temptations songbook. Foremost among those is "Doo Doo Doo Doo Doo (Heartbreaker)." Jagger's vocals betray a deep affinity for David Ruffin and Dennis Edwards, two of the great baritone leads from the Temptations. In addition to "Angie" the epic ballad "Winter" shows a form that would reappear on their records for many years. The albums' visuals are notable for their blending of the beautiful and, seemingly, grotesque. Photographed by David Bailey, all the band members seen in head shots with their heads wrapped in translucent scarf-like cloths. While Jagger, whose face adorns the cover, appears more androgynous than ever, the image of Keith Richards makes it looks as if he's self-immolating.

The 1973 Tour of Europe demonstrated that no amount of negative press was hurled at the band; their drawing power was not diminished. Even with the notable exclusion of France and Italy, the tour is another giant undertaking. There are 42 shows in 21 cities in nine countries that fall, including a return to Great Britain. A concert recording from Forest National in Brussels, Belgium is electrifying in its intensity. They are as tight as any band could wish to be. Soaring above it is the mellifluous lead guitar work of Mick Taylor. His solo during "Street Fighting Man" takes the band to some mythical place in the East where John Coltrane and Ravi Shankar play rock and roll. In the backline, Nicky Hopkins, after four years of touring, is replaced on keyboards by Billy Preston. A child prodigy who has played with such greats as Mahalia Jackson and Little Richard, as well as being the only person to receive billing on a Beatles record, Preston also has his own successful solo career. He does double-duty on the tour as his own group is one of the opening acts.

With Goats Head Soup still riding high, the Rolling Stones start recording the next record in Munich, West Germany. "Doo Doo Doo Doo Doo (Heartbreaker)" becomes the second single released from Goats Head Soup. It peaks at Number 15 in the U.S while failing to make the U.K. charts. Keith Richards, who is essentially living in Ron Wood's home in London, is helping Wood with his first solo record. A track, "It's Only Rock and Roll" – with Jagger and David Bowie on vocals, Andy Newmark on drums and Willie Weeks on bass, along with Richards and Wood – will find its way onto the next Stones album.

With no plans to tour, the Rolling Stones use 1974 to rest, reassemble and create again. Recording continues in Munich with Billy Preston, Nicky Hopkins and percussionist Ray Cooper all joining in.

Bill Wyman also starts work in Los Angeles on what will be the first solo record from a Rolling Stone. He enlists a remarkable roster of American musician including Dr. John, Leon Russell and Little Feat's Lowell George. Session also take place in Miami. Monkey Grip is well received and sheds a new light on the stoic bassist.

In April, the long-awaited film of the 1972 tour opens in New York for a limited run. It will play in several U.S. cities, appearing to be a "touring film" complete with concert style sound. Although it's a suitable document, and the band is in tremendous form, it is nowhere near the quality of motion picture that Gimme Shelter was. The Stones, however, are on to something. They know that their reputation as a live act and a hot ticket leaves many fans in many parts of the world simply unable to see them. Concert films, pay-per-view television specials and live records will become a key part of their economic model in the coming years.

With a new record complete, the band set the promotional machine in motion. With no tour dates planned, the Stones film a promotional clip for the title cut and first single, "It's Only Rock and Roll." The single is released in July. The song is essentially the same as it was cut six months before at Ron Wood's house. However, the song bears only songwriting credit for Jagger/Richards and the track, the Rolling Stones. In the promo film, the band is clad in sailor suits and mime along to the track as they are slowly enveloped in foamy suds. Perhaps it was a more appetizing prospect than another tour. In any event, the song is immediately, and rightfully, pegged as an anthem. It's the rare type of song that actually becomes part of common language. The single does respectably on the charts, Number 10 in the U.K. and Number 19 in the U.S, but it doesn't matter. "It's Only Rock and Roll" joins "Satisfaction," "Jumping Jack Flash" and "Brown Sugar" as true rock and roll classics.

In October, the album It's Only Rock and Roll was released. The time spent traveling the world and recording in so many locales over the last five years seems to all play out on the record. At first, Jamaica was merely a place to record. Now Keith Richards owned a home there. "Luxury" was their first real stab at reggae and they did it with their own thumbprint in place and still remained true to its spirit. Soul balladry like "Till the Next Goodbye" and "If Your Really Want to Be My Friend" would be equally believable if they were credited Gamble and Huff instead of Jagger and Richards. "Dance Little Sister" and "If You Can't Rock Me" are the stuff that the Stones have always been made of. And if any proof was needed that the Stones were not following a formula, look no further than the spookiness of "Fingerprint File." Soon after the album is released, a cover of the Temptations 1966 hit "Ain't Too Proud to Beg" becomes the second single. It is the first time since "Little Red Rooster" in 1964 that they release a cover song as a single. "Ain't Too Proud to Beg" hits Number 17 in the U.S. but doesn't make the U.K. charts.

With no tour, the Rolling Stones return to Munich to set about work on the next album. There is a change, though. Mick Taylor informs the group that he is leaving the band. The news is met with some dismay but it's not a complete surprise. Taylor was the odd man out in the Rolling Stones. He was a bit younger and his personality was far more subdued than some of the others. Musically, he couldn't have joined at a more opportune moment. His tenure with the Rolling Stones is considered by many to be the high-water mark for the band's recorded creativity and power as a live act. It's everything else – the media scrutiny, police hassles, fan frenzy— that makes it intolerable. Mick Taylor walked away and the Stones have to, once again, find a new lead guitarist.

72 The Glimmer Twins take the spotlight. Mick Jagger and Keith Richards in concert in Europe in 1973. Their public persona as musical partners would face serious challenges in the Seventies.

80-81 At one time, one of the world's most eligible bachelors, Mick Jagger takes the matrimonial plunge with Bianca Perez Morena de Marcias in St. Tropez on May 21, 1971.

85 Did someone lose their boots? Mick Jagger in 1970.

86 Hello, Sailor! The Rolling Stones in 1974 on the set of their promotional film for "It's Only Rock and Roll (But I Like It)." Director Michael Lindsay-Hogg directed this and more than 20 other promotional clips for the Stones.

88-89 and 89 Bill Wyman and Charlie Watts attended Brian Jones' funeral at St. Mary's Parish Church in Cheltenham on July 10, 1969. Mick Jagger and Marianne Faithfull sent flowers as they were in Australia at the time.

90 and 91 A photo call in Hyde Park. The Rolling Stones introduce their newest member, 21 year-old guitarist Mick Taylor, to the assembled press. Taylor's arrival coincided with an artistically fertile yet deeply troubled period in the group's history.

ROLLINGSTONES

ROLLINGSTONESROLLINGSTONESROLLINGSTONES
ROLLINGSTONESROLLINGSTONESROLLINGSTONES
ROLLINGSTONESROLLINGSTONESROLLINGSTONES
ROLLINGSTONESROLLINGSTONESROLLINGSTONES
ROLLINGSTONESROLLINGSTONESROLLINGSTONES
ROLLINGSTONESROLLINGSTONESROLLINGSTONES
ROLLINGSTONESROLLINGSTONESROLLINGSTONES
ROLLINGSTONESROLLINGSTONESROLLINGSTONES
ROLLINGSTONESROLLINGSTONESROLLINGSTONES
ROLLINGSTONESROLLINGSTONESROLLINGSTONES

HYDE PARK

92 and 92-93 The Rolling Stones perform for nearly 300,000 people in Hyde Park on July 5, 1969. Brian Jones' recent death turned the event into a makeshift memorial.

94 Chuck Berry, arguably the biggest influence on the Rolling Stones, pays a courtesy call backstage at Madison Square Garden in 1969.

94-95 Keith Richards and Mick Jagger on stage at Madison Square Garden in New York City in 1969. The performances on the 1969 U.S. tour, their first in three years, were triumphant.

you got the silver

96-97 In the years prior to the 1969 U.S. tour, the Rolling Stones rarely performed for more than 45 minutes. The manner in which rock concerts were presented had changed dramatically in the interim and two hour long shows were now expected of a headliner.

ROLLINGSTONES

98-99 The Rolling Stones returned to the stages of Europe in 1970 for their first extended tour of the continent since 1967.

100 and 100-101 Like the 1969 U.S. tour, the 1970 tour of Europe proved the Rolling Stones to be at the height of the powers and virtually without peer.

ROLLINGSTONESROLLINGSTONESROLLINGSTONES
ROLLINGSTONESROLLINGSTONESROLLINGSTONES
ROLLINGSTONESROLLINGSTONESROLLINGSTONES
ROLLINGSTONESROLLINGSTONES

ROLLINGSTONESROLLINGSTONESROLLINGSTONES
ROLLINGSTONESROLLINGSTONESROLLINGSTONES
ROLLINGSTONESROLLINGSTONESROLLINGSTONES
ROLLINGSTONESROLLINGSTONESROLLINGSTONES
ROLLINGSTONESROLLINGSTONESROLLINGSTONES
ROLLINGSTONESROLLINGSTONESROLLINGSTONES
ROLLINGSTONESROLLINGSTONESROLLINGSTONES

102 and 103 The Rolling Stones board a boat in the harbor at Hamburg for a photo opportunity and press conference prior to their four shows in Germany in September 1970.

105 Mick Jagger, resplendent in pink satin, blowing harp in concert. Keith Richards has frequently expressed his admiration for Jagger's prowess on the instrument.

"PEOPLE OFTEN GET THE WRONG
IMPRESSION OF MICK
THE CLEVER BUSINESSMAN
IS JUST ONE SIDE OF MICK
THE OTHER SIDE
IS THE SAME
AS THE REST OF US
A TRUE ROCKER!"

RON WOOD

106-107 The Rolling Stones appearing again on Top of the Pops in 1971. They performed three songs from their new release, Sticky Fingers.

107 Mick Jagger and Keith Richards in concert. As the decade progressed, Jagger began to use several different designers for his stage clothing.

108-109 The Rolling Stones 1971 U.K. tour was their first in their homeland since 1966. At the end of the trek, the band relocated to France as tax exiles.

110 Less clothes and more make-up. Mick Jagger, seen here at Empire Pool, Wembley in 1973, set the pace for all lead singers.

"THE ONLY PERFORMANCE
THAT MAKES IT
THAT MAKES IT ALL THE WAY
IS THE ONE
THAT ACHIEVES
MADNESS"

MICK JAGGER

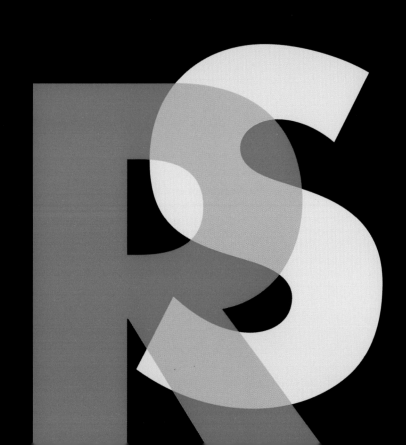

112-113 The Rolling Stones kicked off their tour of Australia, New Zealand and Hong Kong with two dates in Hawaii.

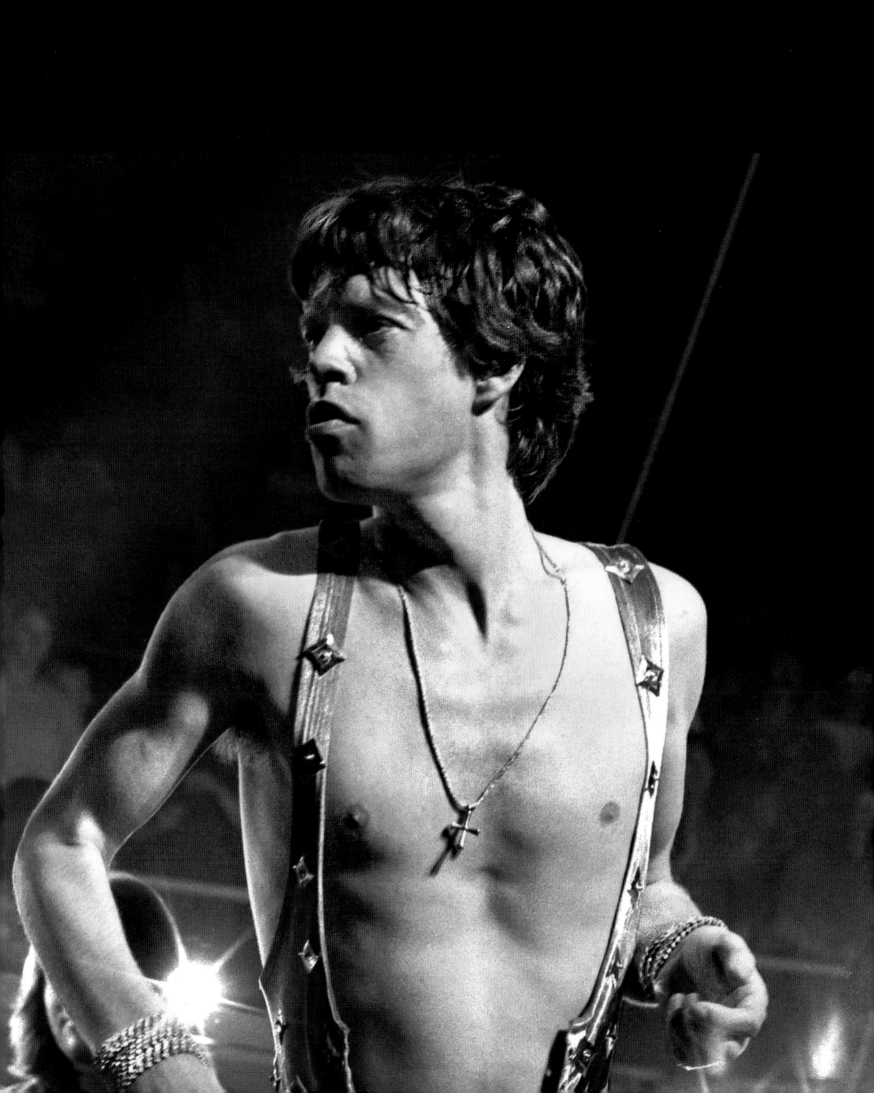

114 and 115 Guitarist Mick Taylor brought to the Rolling Stones a tremendous proficiency at lead guitar. By extension, it allowed Keith Richards to dig deeper into his role as rhythm guitarist.

116 Is it glimmer or glam? Dressed in a jumpsuit designed by Ossie Clark, Mick Jagger prepares to shower the audience with flowers.

117 Is this stage big enough for more than one spotlight? Charlie Watts, at rear, keeps the fire burning in the engine room as the Rolling Stones kick off a tour in Hawaii.

1975-1982

When the Whip
Comes Down

MADE IN THE SHADE
BLACK AND BLUE
LOVE YOU LIVE
SOME GIRLS
TIME WAITS FOR NO ONE
EMOTIONAL RESCUE
SUCKING IN THE SEVENTIES
TATTOO YOU
STILL LIFE

With the Rolling Stones on the hunt for a new lead guitarist, odds makers and prognosticators of all stripes started a frenzied speculation about who would be the newest Rolling Stone. The names of many capable players – Jeff Beck, Mick Ronson, Rory Gallagher and Peter Frampton – were just few to be bandied about. Without a second guitar player in the fold, the Stones set up in Rotterdam with the Mighty Mobile to begin cutting tracks. Along for the sessions were Billy Preston on keys and Ollie E. Brown on percussion. In Rotterdam, Gallagher and Beck each jam with the band and see if the feeling is there. Two lesser-known Americans are also invited test the waters. Harvey Mandel was a Chicago-bred guitarist by way of the Bay Area who was reared in the blues like his contemporary, Mike Bloomfield. Wayne Perkins was from Alabama and had mostly been a studio guitarist. In addition to many Muscle Shoals sessions, he most notably played on the Chris Blackwell-produced overdubbing sessions for Bob Marley and the Wailers Island Records debut, Catch a Fire. Perkins had recorded with the Stones in Munich in December 1974. The sessions move to Munich and conclude in April.

By springtime, Ron Wood had become the unknown front-runner for the position. A founder of the Birds (not to be confused with the Byrds), he later played bass in the first incarnation of the Jeff Beck Group and, along with Rod Stewart, transitioned the Small Faces to the Faces. A longtime friend of the band, Wood had become closer with Keith Richards and Mick Jagger over the preceding years. In the field of candidates, there were guitarists of greater technical ability than Wood. He possessed the personal chemistry with Richards that was truly needed to keep the Rolling Stones vibrant. In mid-April, Wood is announced as the touring guitarist for the Rolling Stones forthcoming American tour but would not be leaving the Faces. At least for the time being.

Ron Wood's first appearance with the Stones takes place on the back of a flat-bed truck rolling along Fifth Avenue in New York City as the Stones announce the dates and ticket sales for the 1975 Tour of the Americas. The original itinerary scheduled the band to make their South American debut with shows in Brazil and Venezuela. Eventually those dates were scrapped, along with shows in Mexico. Made in the Shade, the first greatest hits package on their own Rolling Stones Records, comes out just before the tour. Within weeks, ABKCO releases Metamorphosis, a contractual obligation of studio scraps that never were intended to see the light of day.

The extravaganza aspect was considerably upped by the custom-made lotus-shaped stage. One version of the stage featured hydraulic petals that opened as the band appeared to the strains of Aaron Copeland's "Fanfare for the Common Man." Whether this song was picked for the sake of irony is still unclear as common is not a term often associated with the Rolling Stones. Never ones to be demure, the stage also featured a 20-foot long inflatable phallus. In a year when Led Zeppelin and the Who also toured the U.S., there was no mistaking which band went to greater lengths for the sake of showmanship.

Legendary among this 10-week run was the series of dates at the Forum in Los Angeles. Occurring right in the middle of the tour, the band was burning on all cylinders. The shows were videotaped but never released.

At the end of the tour, the Stones dispersed but Ron Wood reassumed his spot with the Faces and headed back on the road. At the end of the year, Rod Stewart would announce his departure form the Faces and it would appear that Wood has another gig in his pocket. Bill Wyman began work on a second solo record.

In early 1976, the Rolling Stones meet with Ron Wood to discuss formalizing their relationship. When the band goes to Clearwater, Florida in February to shoot the cover for with the forthcoming record, Wood is included. The announcement that he is joining the band comes out in February. Bill Wyman's second solo album, Stone Alone, comes out about the same time.

In April Rolling Stones Records released Black and Blue. The album only contains eight cuts, half of which are over five minutes in length. Sonically, it's a departure from its predecessor, It's Only Rock and Roll. The record delves deeper into groove based songs. The presence of reggae and funk is sewn through many of the cuts. This is partially attributable to Billy Preston's contributions. His own solo career, which paralleled his tenure in the Stones, produced a number of great funk hits. The scope of his talent is also seen on "Melody," probably the closest the Stones have ever been to jazz. The opener "Hot Stuff" was straight-on funk with a simmering island-inspired undercurrent, as was "Hey Negrita." A cover of the 1971 Eric Donaldson reggae classic "Cheery Oh Baby," is another in that vein. Rock and roll was not, however, missing from this record. Both "Crazy Mama" and "Hand of Fate" deliver the chunky guitar rock that made the band's name. The two ballads are notable for a few reasons; "Memory Motel" is the first Rolling Stones recording on which none of the band play guitar. Both parts are supplied by Wayne Perkins and Harvey Mandel. "Fool to Cry" is the first single from Black and Blue and it's their highest achieving U.K single in three years. It peaks at Number 6. In the U.S., the same single stalls at Number 10. The advertising campaign for the record raised the ire of several women's groups who objected, understandably, to the image of a bound and bruised woman straddling the record cover.

Prior to the tour, Keith Richards narrowly avoids death when he falls asleep behind the wheel of his car which careens off the road and is totaled. The police arrive and, upon searching the vehicle and Richards, arrest him on various drug charges.

A new studio record on the streets usually means a tour is not far behind, and the Rolling Stones take to Europe for the late spring and the early summer of 1976. Past legal problems had kept Keith Richards from entering France but that was now behind them and the band could play Paris as well as rehearse in the country. For the first time, the Rolling Stones perform in Spain and Yugoslavia. The tour wrapped at the end of June but the final show of the year was a massive festival gig at Knebworth Park in Hertfordshire. Technical problems delayed their set time to after 11:00 PM but the Stones rose to the occasion and played for more than two hours.

In the fall, tapes of the past two tours are being reviewed for a future live record. Work will continue in the New Year, but not without more trouble.

Keith Richards went to trial in January for drug possession charges relating to his auto accident the previous May. He is found guilty of and pays a total of £1000 in fines and costs. Rolling Stones Records cuts a new deal with EMI for international distribution. This is the quiet before the storm.

In February, the Rolling Stones go to Toronto, Canada to play a couple club gigs with the intension of recording the shows to augment the live record they cut on the recent '75 U.S. and '76 European tours. On February 24, Keith Richards, Anita Pallenberg and their son Marlon, fly in days after the others had arrived. Canadian customs take to giving Anita's numerous bags and luggage a close inspection and discover hashish, heroin residue and various sorts of drug paraphernalia. Anita is arrested and booked, then released the same night based on her promise to appear in court.

Within days, the hammer falls on Keith. The Royal Canadian Mounted Police have had the Rolling Stones in their sights since arriving and Keith is arrested after his room is searched. The RCMP discovers enough heroin to charge Keith with trafficking. Under Canadian statutes, Keith faces a minimum of seven years behind bars if convicted of the lightest of the charges. At worst, it's a life conviction. His chances of walking away, as he did in January, looked poor. He posts bail, surrenders his passport and rejoins the rehearsals.

Amid the tabloid maelstrom that Keith and Anita's busts have created, the Stones rehearse in advance of their gigs. On March 4, the band plays at the intimate El Mocambo located on Spadina Avenue, near the University of Toronto. Canadian rockers April Wine, a local favorite who will become a national institution, are the billed attraction but the secret had been spoiled. Adding to the madness and press frenzy, Margaret Trudeau, the wife of Canada's Prime Minister, Pierre Trudeau, is seen in the company of the band and attends the shows.

In the packed club the Stones play some hits but really lean on their roots. According to Bill Wyman, the band started "very loose" but gained their footing as show goes on. The second show is stronger and the results, as heard on side three of Love You Live, are stunning. The four songs chosen to be released come straight from their 1963 set list. Playing Chicago blues that they worshiped in their early days, they tackle songs made famous by their heroes - Chuck Berry, Bo Diddley, Howlin' Wolf and Muddy Waters. In spite of the persistent shitstorm swirling about them, the Stones are consistently in the groove. As Jagger bares his fiercest guttural call on "Mannish Boy," Billy Preston provides the perfect response. "Crackin' Up" is a showcase for, what Rolling Stone Magazine calls, Charlie Watts' "totally cool drumming" and Ollie Brown's tasteful percussion. Ron Wood's prowess on slide guitar makes the "Little Red Rooster" truly "crow for days." And on "Around and Around," Keith Richards blazes a note perfect solo that may be his finest on record.

With the two shows wrapped, all but Richards and Pallenberg beat a hasty retreat from Toronto. The Canadians still hold their passports and both have court dates to make. In early April, they finally leave Toronto for the U.S. and Keith enters a rehab facility to kick his heroin habit.

Rolling Stones Record renews its North American distribution deal with WEA and announces that longtime record business veteran Earl McGrath will take over as label president for Marshall Chess. In September, the third live album from the Rolling Stones, Love You Live is released. Featuring artwork by Andy Warhol, the tracks are mostly taken from the 1976 Paris shows with one from London, three from the 1975 North American tour and the aforementioned El Mocambo gig.

In October, the band regrouped at EMI's Pathe'-Marconi Studios, just outside of Paris. With Richards' legal fate still unknown, the band set to work and yield remarkable results. This session, and the one following the New Year, would show the band at another creative peak. Since their last long player, Black and Blue in 1976, punk rock had reset the standards for credibility. So-called "dinosaur" acts like the Stones, Pink Floyd and Led Zeppelin were openly mocked for their wealth and popularity. Rising to the challenge, the Stones shed everything but the core and worked from a sheaf of inspired new compositions. Pathe'-Marconi would become the Rolling Stones main recording base for several years as Olympic Studios in Barnes had been nearly a decade before.

Keith Richards' legal problems continued to linger through 1978. His bust in Canada kept the future of entire operation in limbo, but for the present a new album was still on the docket. Ron Wood's former Faces colleague, Ian McLagan, came aboard to play keyboards for the recording sessions in addition to the ever-present Ian Stewart.

In May, "Miss You" / "Far Away Eyes" came out. The a-side is a seductive disco-inspired slab of a dance song that is met with no small amount of negative reaction. The entire disco movement was engendered a shocking level of animosity from many rock fans. Perhaps it was the fact that much of it came out of gay nightclubs. Or possibly that it didn't resemble much of the "stadium" sort of rock, music which had abandoned its dance roots ages ago. The Rolling Stones always embraced contemporary movements in black music and this was no exception. With rock radio in America snubbing "Miss You," Top 40 took the lead and the song became the Rolling Stones last to Number One. In the U.K. it made it to Number Three. The b-side was a perfect contrast in the form of a sweet country-style ballad. A version with overdubbed fiddle by Doug Kershaw was prepared for country radio but never released.

The 1978 U.S. tour got underway in Lakeland, Florida on June 10 and ran for six weeks. Unlike the 1975 tour which stuck to arenas and stadiums, this tour included small venues like the Palladium in New York City, the Warner Theatre in Washington, D.C. and the Masonic Auditorium in Detroit. A bit of old-time fan frenzy broke out at the Detroit show when a rush of fans climbed a fire escape and gained entry to the hall. Opening many of the shows was ex-Wailer Peter Tosh. He became the first signing to Rolling Stones Records after being personally courted by Mick Jagger.

Some Girls was released as the U.S. tour got underway. The 10 songs are the Rolling Stones in remarkable fighting trim. The recent punk rock movement may have ignited a desire to reconnect with the minimalism of their early records. Tracks like "Lies," "Respectable" and "When the Whip Comes Down" are as fierce and stark as anything they'd previously recorded. The element of autobiography is clear in Keith Richards' vocal turn on "Before They Make Me Run" and Mick Jagger's "Some Girls," which also was the cause for some controversy over Jagger's assertions about the demands and preferences of certain women. Some Girls is a massive hit and is the Rolling Stones best selling non-compilation album in the U.S. with more than 6 million copies sold.

When the tour ends, Richards' trial in Canada looms. Unbeknownst to him, a longtime Canadian fan with which he was acquainted, a blind woman who followed the Stones on tour, makes a personal appeal to the judge who is trying the case. Richards pleads guilty to a lesser charge of possession and avoids jail. He is, however, subject to probation, continued treatment for his addiction and must play a benefit concert for the blind in Canada within six months. Whether another person in the same situation would have fared as well is subject to speculation.

Recording for the follow-up to Some Girls began soon after the New Year. The whole group gathered at Compass Point Studios in the Bahamas. Those sessions as well as others from Paris would make up the new record.

The Keith Richards Benefit Concert in Oshawa, Ontario, Canada was an instant sellout. Two shows were scheduled for April 22. Ron Wood, who had signed a solo deal with CBS Records the previous year, was about to release Gimme Some Neck. He and Richards combined forces with their old sax playing pal Bobby Keys, Ian McLagan on keys, jazz bassist Stanley Clarke and Joseph "Zigaboo" Modeliste from the Meters on drums to form the New Barbarians. The Rolling Stones also performed at both shows but were not billed. It is their only appearance of the year. The New Barbarians set out on their U.S. tour playing a mix of Wood, Richards and Rolling Stones songs in arenas around the U.S. They play just one U.K. date anchoring the under card for Led Zeppelin's gig at Knebworth.

The second compilation from the Stones on their own label is a U.K Only release. Time Waits for No One takes its title from a track on It's Only Rock and Roll. The collection itself is a companion of sorts to Made in the Shade but, overall, it's not one for the ages.

There were no tour plans for the Rolling Stones for 1980. A new record did need to be made, however. Since 1977, there was a tremendous amount of material from sessions in Paris, the Bahamas, Los Angeles and New York. Emotional Rescue, the single and album came out in June. The single was a bass guitar driven jam with a disco tinge emphasized by Mick Jagger's falsetto. Again, the backlash against this aspect of the Stones' style left some of their fan base wondering. It was, in hindsight, just another aspect of the music that always captivated the band. The rest of the record featured searing blues ("Down in the Hole"), a ballad ("Indian Girl") and more than enough straight on rockers ("She's So Cold," "Summer Romance" and "Where the Boys Go"). The trend of higher charting in America continued with "Emotional Rescue" making it to Number Three in the U.S. and Number Nine in the U.K. The album hit Number One in both countries. "She's So Cold" was released as the second single but didn't match the success of the first track.

After many years of wrangling, negotiations and discussions Cocksucker Blues, Robert Frank's backstage documentary of the 1972 tour, finally has its world premiere at the Whitney Museum of American Art in New York City. By agreement with the Stones, the film can only be screened when Frank is present and attending.

Perhaps it's another contractual obligation, but the Rolling Stones release their third compilation in early 1981. This time, however, it's not just a set of hits, though it does share some tracks with Time Waits for No One from 1979. Sucking in the Seventies, a bold title no matter how much self-deprecation a group possessed, is a collections of some a-sides, some b-sides and a previously unreleased live track.

The bigger project is Tattoo You. It's clear that the Rolling Stones are in a uniquely identifiable era within their own story. Where Some Girls was a return to form and Emotional Rescue was a pop hit that lacked some bite, Tattoo You was a surprise triumph. It was, in many ways, the record least likely to be a big deal. Some of the tracks date as far back to 1968 and several actually have Mick Taylor clearly on them, despite his lack of credit. The record is sequenced in a very deliberate manner; side one is all rock and roll, side two is soul and slower tempo fare. At first glance it seems this sort of musical segregation is counterintuitive. It's certainly unlike anything the Stones have done before. What it does do is accent the themes that have always defined Rolling Stones.

"Start Me Up" is the lead single. Like several of its predecessors, the track is a true rock anthem and an immediate classic. It's another major hit for the band (Number Two U.S. and Number Six U.K.) as is the album (Number 1 U.S. and Number Two U.K.)

Although it's called a North American Tour, the 1981 trek only plays the U.S. Perhaps feelings in Canada were still a bit raw or there was no sense in adding to ones own problems if they can be avoided. The tour is played mostly in stadiums with a few arenas and only one theater. The Stones pioneer a new aspect in the concert business. The 1981 tour becomes the first major tour to have a sponsor. Fragrance maker Jovan reportedly paid one million dollars to have their name associated with the tour. The band members themselves make no personal endorsement of the product.

Film director Hal Ashby, best known for Harold and Maude, Shampoo and Being There, captures performances at Sun Devil Stadium in Tempe, Arizona and Brendan Byrne Arena in New Jersey for a forthcoming feature length theatrical film.

The final show of the tour is another pioneering event as the Rolling Stones go the way of boxing matches and telecast their concert from Hampton, Virginia as a pay-per-view event.

Taking the maxim "if it ain't broke, don't fix it" to heart, 1982 looked a lot like 1981 for the Rolling Stones. The major differences being there is no new studio record and the touring market is Europe. It's been six years since the Stones last played Europe and demand was intense. The audience numbers triple the amount of the 1976 tour. The biggest change is keyboardist Ian McLagan is out and he is replaced by Chuck Leavell. A friend of Ian Stewart, Leavell is a native of Alabama who joined the Allman Brothers Band following the death of Duane Allman. He left a few years later and formed his own band, Sea Level. Leavell became an intricate part of the Rolling Stones touring band although that really wouldn't come to full fruition for several years. Sill Life, a live record from the 1981 record was released and the pattern of a live record to follow a Rolling Stones tour is established.

118 The arrival of the salaried Stone. Ron Wood takes a busman's holiday from his day gig with the Faces and accompanies the Rolling Stones on tour.

123 Keith Richards keeps his footing on a the back of a moving truck as the Rolling Stones roll down Fifth Avenue in New York City to announce their 1975 Tour of the Americas.

128-129 Keith Richards and Ron Wood are the picture of rock and roll luxury as they chat aboard their chartered jet during the 1975 Tour of the Americas.

when the whip comes down

130-131 Mick Jagger and touring keyboard player Billy Preston keep up on current events on the Stones plane.

132 and 132-133 The Rolling Stones entertain the assembled press and a group of surprised fans when they perform unannounced on the back of a flatbed truck in New York City, May 1, 1975.

134-135 Don't forget to stretch. Mick Jagger gets some assistance for his pre-show exercise routine backstage in 1975.

135 Writer Lisa Robinson goes outside the normal call of journalistic duty to help bassist Bill Wyman work out some muscle tension.

136-137 and 137 Guitarist Ron Wood gets in tune and drummer Charlie Watts warms up prior to taking the stage.

138 and 138-139 Keith Richards find time for some quiet reflection backstage, right, before digging into the makeup kit and applying his war paint for the show.

ROLLINGSTONESROLLINGSTONESROLLINGSTONES
ROLLINGSTONESROLLINGSTONESROLLINGSTONES
ROLLINGSTONESROLLINGSTONESROLLINGSTONES
ROLLINGSTONESROLLINGSTONESROLLINGSTONES
ROLLINGSTONESROLLINGSTONESROLLINGSTONE
ROLLINGSTONESROLLINGSTONESROLLINGSTONES
ROLLINGSTONESROLLINGSTONESROLLINGSTONES
ROLLINGSTONESROLLINGSTONESROLLINGSTONES
ROLLINGSTONESROLLINGSTONESROLLINGSTONES
ROLLINGSTONESROLLINGSTONESROLLINGSTONES
ROLLINGSTONESROLLINGSTONESROLLINGSTONES
ROLLINGSTONESROLLINGSTONESROLLINGSTONES
ROLLINGSTONESROLLINGSTONESROLLINGSTONE
ROLLINGSTONESROLLINGSTONESROLLINGST
ROLLINGSTONESROLLINGSTON
ROLLINGSTONESROLLING
ROLLINGSTONESRO
ROLLINGSTONESROLLING
ROLLINGSTONESROLLINGSTON
ROLLINGSTONESROLLING
ROLLINGSTONESROLLINGSTONES
ROLLINGSTONESRO
ROLLINGSTONESROLLIN

140-141 The Rolling Stones on stage at the Convention Center in San Antonio, Texas for the second show of the 1975 tour. Local authorities threaten obscenity charges if the Stones use their giant inflatable penis stage prop during the show.

142 and 143 In the air or on the ground, Mick Jagger's position as the best showman in rock and roll has rarely been the subject of debate.

144-145 The Rolling Stones 1975 edition on their custom built stage. Left to right: Billy Preston, Ron Wood, Mick Jagger, Ollie E. Brown, Charlie Watts, Keith Richards and Bill Wyman.

ROLLINGSTON ES-ROLLINGSTON ES-ROLLINGSTON ES-ROLLINGSTON ES-ROLLINGSTON ES

146 and 146-147 Mick Jagger mugging it up on stage with Keith Richards in Europe in 1976, left, and in the U.S. in 1975, right.

148 Ron Wood catches some spray as Mick Jagger turns his articulated confetti cannon on a willing audience during the 1976 European tour.

148-149 Maybe he learned this one at the taping of the Rock and Roll Circus. Mick Jagger gives his insurance adjuster fits as he swings over the audience.

150-151 Ron Wood appears carefree as he pushes the barriers of his own multi-tasking skills without getting out of bed.

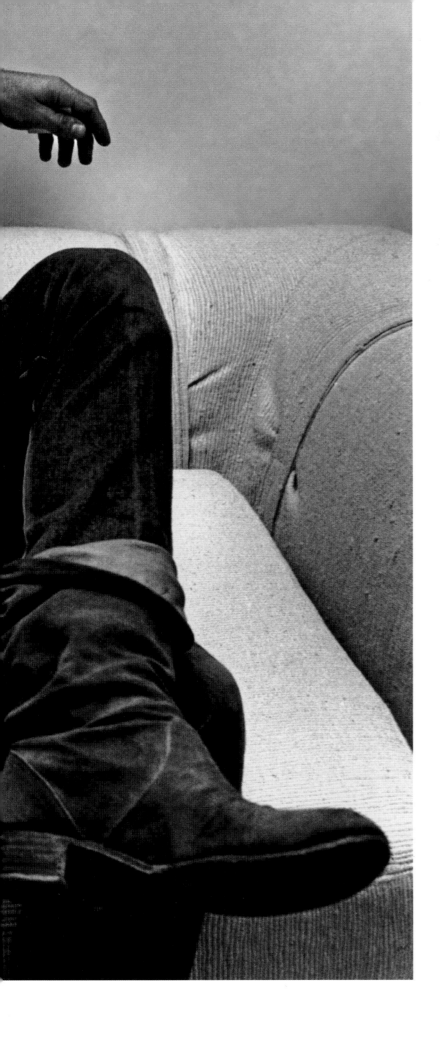

152-153 Keith Richards looking fit and healthy, despite the cigarette, in 1980.

154 and 155 Charlie Watts, seen at left in the Sixties, and above in 1975, has been the guiding force behind the Rolling Stones visual design aesthetic.

156 Keith Richards, en route to the launch party for Emotional Rescue, takes to the streets of New York armed with a bottle of Jack Daniels Tennessee Whiskey.

"I SAY GOOD LUCK TO PEOPLE
WHO WANT TO EMULATE ME
BUT THEY BETTER REALIZE
WHAT THEY'RE GETTING INTO
THEY BETTER KNOW THAT THERE'S
MORE TO THIS THAN ATTITUDE
IT'S ABOUT THE MUSIC
IT'S ABOUT THE BLUES
THAT'S WHAT
SUSTAINS ME"

KEITH RICHARDS

ROLLINGSTONES
ROLLINGSTONES
ROLLINGSTONES

ROLLING
STONES

158-159 and 159 For the dates on the Rolling Stones 1981 US tour, the group played on a stage decorated to resemble their lips and tongue logo. Runway ramps and a cherry picker allowed Mick Jagger to work close to the crowd.

161 Mick Jagger bares skin in Canada at the Rolling Stones/New Barbarians concert in Oshawa, Ontario, April 22, 1979. This was the only occasion where the Stones and the New Barbarians shared a bill.

"I AM NOT A LIBRARIAN OF MY OWN WORK IT'S A GOOD THING NOT TO BE INVOLVED WITH WHAT YOU HAVE DONE"

MICK JAGGER

162-163 Mick Jagger and Ron Wood put their heads together as the Rolling Stones play a show to pay back Keith Richards' debt to the Canadian justice system in Oshawa, Ontario, April 22, 1979.

164 and 165 Ron Wood, right, recruited his Rolling Stones band mate, Keith Richards, left, along with Stanley Clarke, Bobby Keys, Joseph Modeliste and Ian McLagan to tour as the New Barbarians in 1979.

when the whip comes down

166-167 Keith Richards performing "Little T&A" on the 1981 U.S tour. It was the only song Richards sang lead on for the whole tour.

168 and 169 Mick Jagger climbs aboard a cherry picker to elevate above the audience during the 1981 U.S. tour.

1983-1993

Winning Ugly

UNDERCOVER
REWIND
DIRTY WORK
STEEL WHEELS
SINGLES COLLECTION-
THE LONDON YEARS
FLASHPOINT
JUMP BACK

Twenty years was an unthinkable lifespan for a rock and roll group. The very nature of rock and roll was transient, at least according to the accepted wisdom. There was no precedent for any of this. There were many vocal groups from the Fifties who still performed but they were just that, live acts existing on a reputation established decades before with no possibility of making an artistic or commercial impact on any large scale. The Rolling Stones were different. Their career had continued to grow and prosper. Rumors of a "final" Rolling Stones tour had been aired in the press since 1966. At this point, it looked like it might be true. At the end of the 1982 tour, a break was needed. After living in each others back pocket for two decades, relationships between the band members, particularly Jagger and Richards, were frayed.

Hal Ashby's movie of the 1981 tour, Let's Spend the Night Together, premiered in New York in February. The following weekend it opened around the U.S. and pulled in a respectable $1.3 million. In March it opened in the U.K.

Rolling Stones Records distribution deal was up with Atlantic and EMI. CBS Records, now owned by Sony Corporation, was aggressively pursuing the band. Their value as a superstar group would be a feather in the cap of label president Walter Yetnikoff. In August, the Rolling Stones sign a new deal with CBS reportedly worth $28 million dollars. It is one of the most lucrative deals signed in history. Unknown to the other members of the Stones is that the pact includes a solo deal for Mick Jagger.

For the new record, the band starts mostly from scratch with new sessions at Compass Point and EMI Studios. There was friction over the musical direction. The resulting album, Undercover, was released in November. An adventurous record, it incorporated more of a dance club sound that previous Rolling Stones albums. Tracks like "Undercover of the Night" and "Too Much Blood" were ready made for club-style remixes and, in fact, received those treatments. For the first time since 1973, the record is co-produced by an outside producer, Chris Kimsey. Sonically, the Stones are expanding their horizons and avoiding the pitfalls of glomming onto trends. Undercover goes into the Top Five in both the U.K. and the U.S. Of the singles released, only the "Undercover of the Night" breaks the Top 10 and that's just in the U.S. This is the final record of current distribution deal.

Bill Wyman and Charlie Watts join a veritable who's-who of British rock in support of ARMS, a charity devoted to Multiple Sclerosis research. It is spearheaded by ex-Faces bassist Ronnie Lane who suffers from the condition. Following two shows in London, the all-star group, including Jimmy Page, Eric Clapton, Jeff Beck, Joe Cocker and many others, does a brief U.S. tour. In 1984, Mick Jagger records a duet with Michael Jackson, "State of Shock," which is included on a new album from the Jacksons. Jagger had also been at work on his first solo album.

In early 1985, the Rolling Stones regroup in Paris to begin work on their first record for CBS/Sony. Shortly after, Jagger's first solo single, not counting "Memo From Turner," comes out, is fairly well received and sells over a million copies in the U.S. Bill Wyman continues to pitch in to help ARMS with the album Willie and the Poor Boys. The collection of blues and rock songs features contributions from Paul Rodgers, Jimmy Page and Chris Rea.

Bob Geldof meets with the Rolling Stones in Paris in an attempt to recruit them for his fundraising initiative to alleviate the hunger crisis in east Africa. Although the whole group does not participate in Live Aid, they are represented notably. Ron Wood and Keith Richards accompany Bob Dylan in a sometime shaky acoustic set. Following them, Mick Jagger and Tina Turner perform with backing from Daryl Hall and John Oates' band. Jagger also cuts a duet of the Motown classic "Dancing in the Streets" with David Bowie which was released as a single to benefit Live Aid.

In December 1985, Ian Stewart died of a heart attack. There was no disputing among the band that his loss was a massive blow. To some, the Rolling Stones were his band and much of the music they made was a direct result of his influence.

Keith Richards is the first inductor at the inaugural Rock and Roll Hall of Fame induction ceremony in New York in January 1986. Suitably, he inducts Chuck Berry.

With a new record ready to go and no plans to tour behind it, the Rolling Stones shoot a video in New York for "Harlem Shuffle," an R&B nugget that was a minor hit for the duo of Bob and Earl in the Sixties.

In February, the Rolling Stones play their only show in a six year span when they come together for an invitation only audience at the 100 Club in London to salute Ian Stewart.

Dirty Work is the first record of new material from the Rolling Stones for CBS/Sony. If tension marked much of Undercover, it was the main theme of this record. Perhaps the indicator is the fact the Ron Wood received three co-writing credits and Chuck Leavell received one. The production is handled by Steve Lilywhite, best known for his work with U2 and XTC. He finds himself in a difficult position. At various points, the songs sound like they could be from Jagger's solo record or a Richards led project that Jagger sang on. Overall, Dirty Work is not considered to be among the Stones' best work although "Had it With You" and "One Hit (to the Body)," two of Wood's co-writes, are memorable. Of the two single released from Dirty Work, "Harlem Shuffle" makes the best chart showing at Number Five.

The rest of the year is full of activity for the members of the Rolling Stones, just not as a group. Keith Richards appears on stage with Chuck Berry and Etta James. He and Ron Wood contribute to Aretha Franklin's version of "Jumpin' Jack Flash." Richards will act as musical director and foil for Berry in a film directed by Taylor Hackford later in the year. Ron Wood sits in with Bob Dylan and Bo Diddley. Mick Jagger works on another solo record and Charlie Watts forms an orchestra. To many observers, the Rolling Stones no longer appear to be a going concern.

1987 brings another solo record from Jagger, Primitive Cool. Keith Richards signs his own solo deal with Virgin Records. The film Hail, Hail Rock and Roll, in which Richards and others back Chuck Berry for a filmed concert is released. Ron Wood and Bo Diddley team up for a U.S. tour which concludes in Miami, Florida at Wood's new nightclub, Woody's on the Beach.

At the Third Annual Rock and Roll Hall of Fame induction ceremony in January 1988, Jagger inducts the Beatles with Ringo Starr, George Harrison and Yoko Ono in attendance. Despite Richards' objections, Jagger mounts a solo tour of Japan and Australia. Wood and Bo Diddley also go to Japan as well as Europe. Richards forms the X-Pensive Winos, a band with Steve Jordan, Charley Drayton, Waddy Wachtel, Ivan Neville and Sarah Dash. The album, Talk is Cheap, receives universal praise and the ensuing tour is a sellout.

It's the Rolling Stones' turn to enter the Rock and Roll Hall of Fame and Jagger, Richards, Wood and Mick Taylor appear together in New York to accept their award from Pete Townshend in January 1989. It also seems to signal the end of tensions between the principles as the Rolling Stones enter the studio again to record a new record. Working again with Chris Kimsey, the sessions take place at George Martin's AIR studios in Montserrat, West Indies. Canadian promoter Michael Cohl signs the band to an exclusive deal guaranteeing them more than they've ever grossed on a tour before. Sponsors are ready to throw money at he Stones and this time major deals are cut with brewers Budweiser in the U.S. and Labatt in Canada. The announcement of the Steel Wheels tour, their first American trek since 1981 is met with a ticket-buying frenzy. Four shows at Shea Stadium in New York, sell out within hours. Because of the money involved, all but one date is played at stadiums. The tour kicks off in Philadelphia in August and wraps in Atlantic City in December with a pay-per-view concert. This time they add a slate of guests including Eric Clapton, John Lee Hooker and Izzy Stradlin and Axl Rose of Guns 'n' Roses. When all is said and done, the tour is the most successful North American tour of all-time bringing in $98 million dollars.

Steel Wheels was a cohesive, solid record. If Jagger and Richards had any lingering issues, they seemed to have cleared them up. The songs and performances are tight with a distinct leaning on rock and roll. Gone is the infatuation with dance music. They do make a point of digging deep in their past and cut parts of "Continental Drift" in Morocco with the Master Musicians of Joujouka, who had been recorded by Brian Jones in 1968. The first single, "Mixed Emotions," did the best in the U.S. reaching Number Five. This would be the final time the Rolling Stones score a Top Ten hit in the U.S. In a career spanning nearly 30 years, firsts are hard to come by. Nonetheless, in 1990 the Rolling Stones finally make their debut in Japan and play 10 sold out shows at the Tokyo Dome. The tour continued onto Europe, where the Stones hadn't performed in eight years. Rechristened the Urban Jungle tour, it was the biggest and most successful tour of Europe by any band. The final show tour took place at

Wembley Stadium. Though no one knew it at the time, it was Bill Wyman's final gig with the Rolling Stones.

Several of the European shows were filmed in the IMAX format, a super-wide screen film format that can only be shown in specially equipped theaters, usually science centers. The film, At the Max opens in 1991. The expected live album, Flashpoint, comes out in April. It contains two "bonus" studio tracks.

With the coffers freshly filled, Rolling Stones scattered to the wind again. Keith Richards regrouped the X-Pensive Winos to cut a new record. Entitled Main Offender, it comes out in October of 1992. In early 1993, Richards takes the band on the road. Mick Jagger releases his third solo album, Wandering Spirit, also in 1993 but doesn't mount a tour. Bill Wyman announces his decision to leave the Rolling Stones. Late in the year, the Rolling Stones hold invitation-only auditions to find a bass player. Unlike 1974 and 1969, they set up and bring in musicians to play with them. Much of the choice lies with Charlie Watts. Ultimately, they give the seat to Darryl Jones, an American who had played with Miles Davis, Sting, Peter Gabriel and Madonna.

170 The Rolling Stones at the debut of Let's Spend the Night Together.

176 The Rolling Stones take a bow in At-

lantic City, New Jersey at the close of their 1989 Steel Wheels tour. The final show was broadcast live and featured special guest performances.

177 Following the 1990 Urban Jungle tour, bassist Bill Wyman decided he would leave the Rolling Stones. The announcement wasn't made official until 1993.

178 and 178-179 When the Rolling Stones were faced with replacing Mick Taylor, many guitarists auditioned but it was Keith Richards who decided that Ron Wood was the right man for the job.

180-181 Charlie Watts and Keith Richards join the celebration as Ron Wood and Jo Howard married on January 2, 1985. Their divorce was finalized in February 2011.

182 and 183 Keith Richards and Mick Jagger show support for their friend and band mate Charlie Watts as he debuts his Big Band at Ronnie Scott's nightclub in London in 1985.

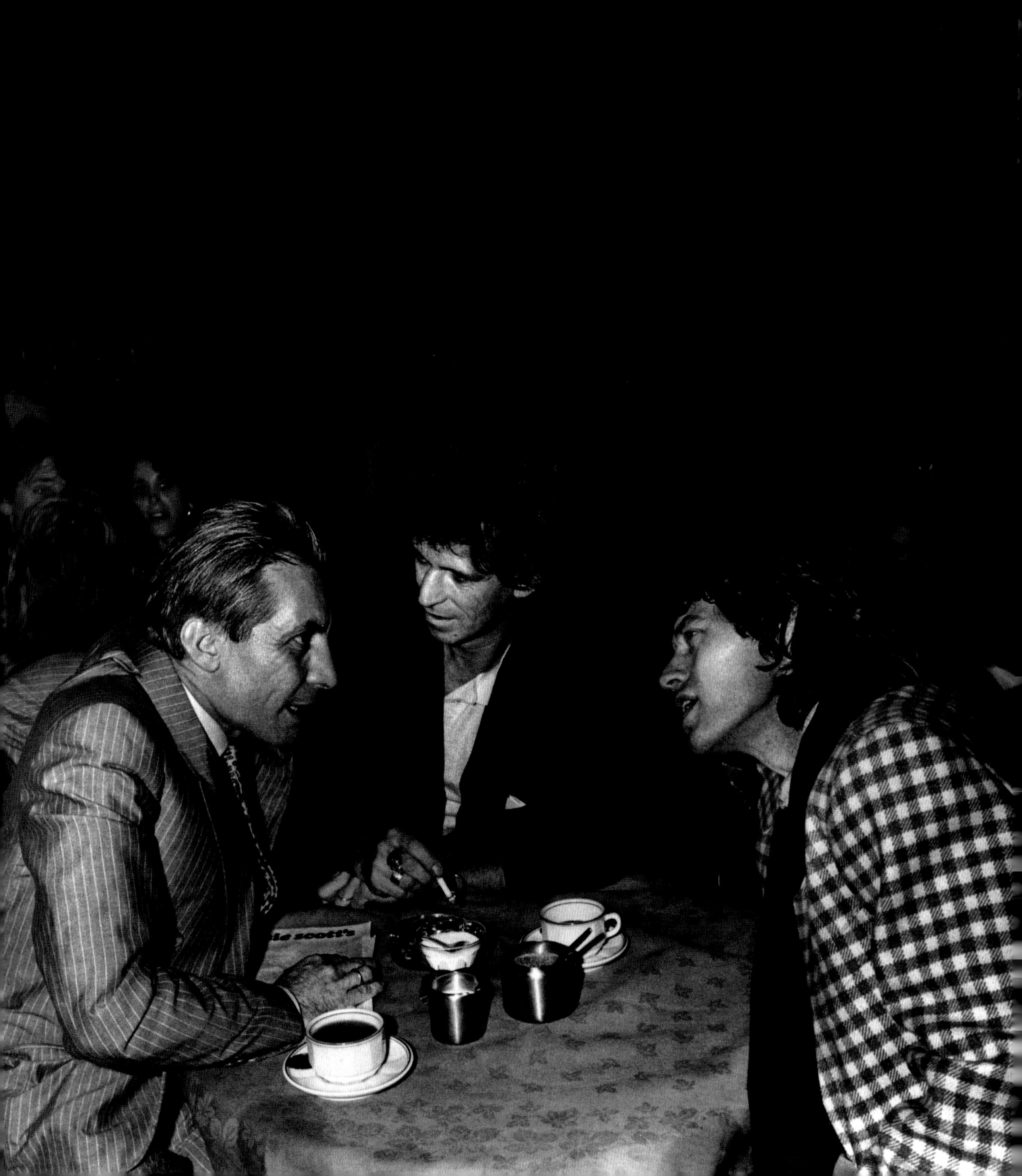

184 and 185 Mick Jagger and Jerry Hall began their relationship in 1977. Prior to meeting Jagger, Hall was a well-known fashion model and had appeared on the cover of Roxy Music's fifth album, Siren. Hall and Jagger are the parents of four children, two girls and two boys. Both daughters followed their mother's footsteps and are models.

ROLLINGSTONESROLLINGSTONES
ROLLINGSTONESROLLINGSTONESROLL
ROLLINGSTONESROLLINGSTONESROLL
ROLLINGSTONESROLLINGSTONESR
ROLLINGSTONESROLLINGSTONESROLLING
ROLLINGSTONESROLLINGSTONESROLLIN
ROLLINGSTONESROLLINGSTONESROLL
ROLLINGSTONESROLLINGSTONESROLL
ROLLINGSTONESROLLINGSTONESR
ROLLINGSTONESROLLINGSTONESROLLING
ROLLINGSTONESROLLINGSTONESROLLINGSTO
LINGSTONESROLLINGSTONESROLLINGSTONES
ROLLINGSTONESROLLINGSTONESROLLINGSTONES
LLINGSTONESROLLINGSTONESROLLINGSTONES
ROLLINGSTONESROLLINGSTONESROLLINGSTONESROLLIN
ROLLINGSTONESROLLINGSTONESROLLINGSTONES
ROLLINGSTONESROLLINGSTONESROLLINGSTONES
LLINGSTONESROLLINGSTONESROLLINGSTONES
ROLLINGSTONESROLLINGSTONESROLLINGSTONES
LINGSTONESROLLINGSTONESROLLINGSTONES
ROLLINGSTONESROLLINGSTONESROLLINGSTONES
ROLLINGSTONESROLLINGSTONESROLLINGSTONES

186-187 Like many other British guitarists, including Keith Richards, Eric Clapton, John Lennon and Pete Townshend, Ron Wood attended art school before becoming a full-time musician. Wood's original artwork and prints have become highly collectable.

188-189 and 189 The Eighties were a particularly dark period for the Rolling Stones. Public airing of personal differences made many observers think the band might not work together again. In 1989, the band regrouped and recorded Steel Wheels. The subsequent tour, with Richards and Jagger seen performing here, became the highest grossing tour ever at the time.

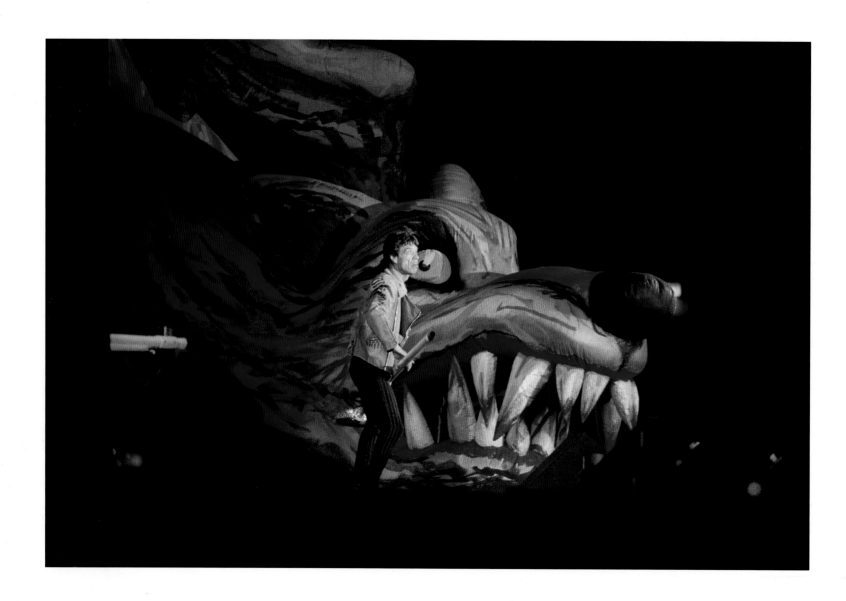

190 The bigger the stage, the bigger the prop. Beginning in 1975, the Rolling Stones incorporated oversize inflatable characters into their live shows. The group loaned the Honky Tonk Women figures to the Rock and Roll Hall of Fame and Museum for their grand opening in 1995.

191 Mick Jagger performs on stage during the Urban Jungle tour in London, 1990.

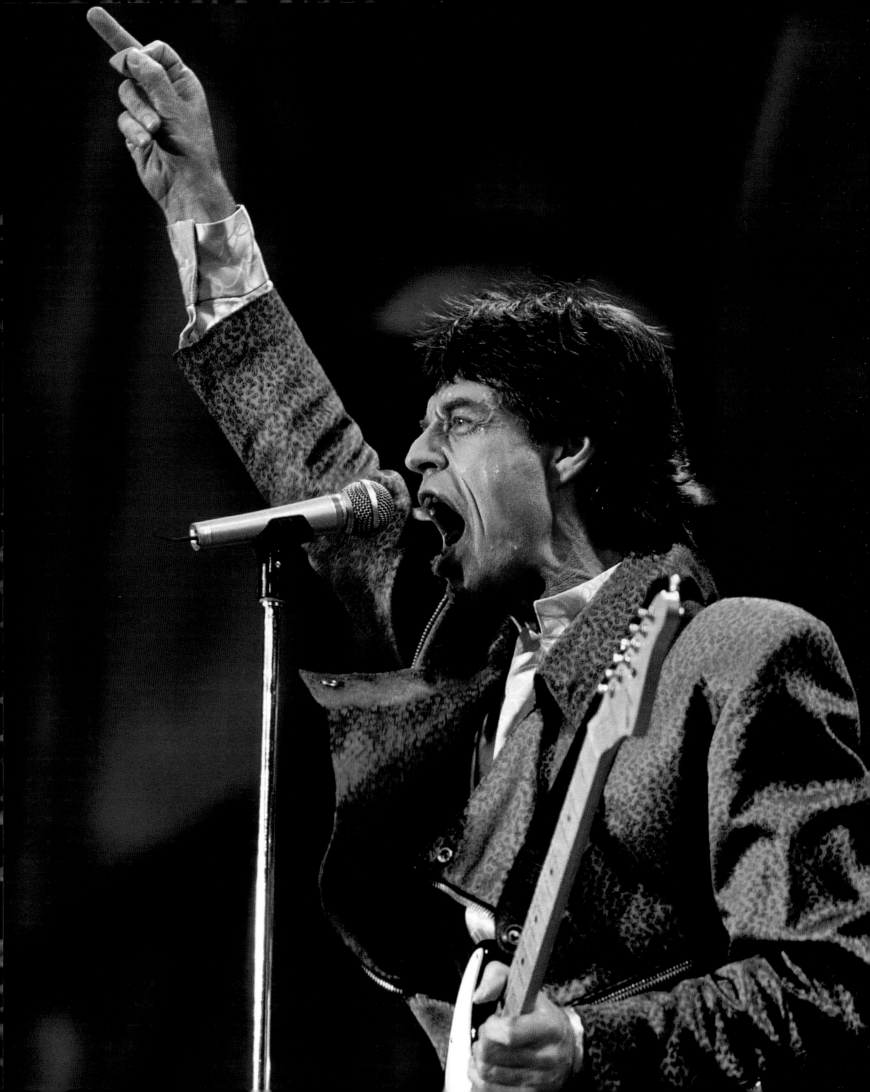

192 Ron Wood breaks out the slide guitar as Keith Richards goes high stepping' on the Steel Wheels tour in Atlantic City, New Jersey.

193 On the Steel Wheels tour, Mick Jagger wraps an arm around Bill Wyman and wrenches a smile out of the famously stoic bass player.

1994-PRESENT

Oh No
Not You Again

VOODOO LOUNGE
STRIPPED
BRIDGES TO BABYLON
NO SECURITY
FORTY LICKS
LIVE LICKS
RARITIES
A BIGGER BANG
SHINE A LIGHT
THE ROLLING STONES SINGLES

Bill Wyman's exit marked the end of one chapter in the story of the Rolling Stones in more ways than seemed possible. Improbably, it marked the beginning of an era where the band was, arguably, more visible than they had ever been before. They would spend the better part of the next 13 years on the road.

For the next studio project the band selected producer Don Was. A musician who had hit records with his band Was (not Was), Was had produced records for Bob Dylan, Iggy Pop and the B-52's. Perhaps his best known production was Bonnie Raitt's 1990 masterpiece Nick of Time. The primary sessions took place at Windmill Lane Studios in Dublin, Ireland with Daryl Jones and Chuck Leavell among the contributing musicians. Was brought a fresh sonic quality to the Rolling Stones without losing their edge or unique qualities. Voodoo Lounge was universally hailed as one of their best albums. It was certainly their most direct and uncluttered records in a while. Charlie Watts takes center stage on much of the record with his consistently driving performances on tracks like "Sparks Will Fly," "Moon Is Up" and "You Got Me Rocking." The Stones reach back to their mid-Sixties sounds in "New Faces" and "Sweethearts Together." The big rock anthems "You Got Me Rocking" and "I Go Wild" reached their full potential when played live. It becomes the Stones first Number One UK since Emotional Rescue in 1980. It reaches Number Two in the US. (Author's note: As the nature of hit radio had changed so greatly over the years, the Rolling Stones made little headway in terms of hit singles at this point in their career. For the exception of particular releases, the position of singles will not be noted any further.)

Working with promoter Michael Cohl again, the band plotted out another massive tour. Also called Voodoo Lounge, the tour is a take-no-prisoners, worldwide campaign. Like the 1981 and 1989 tours, the US leg of the tour starts in late summer and runs through December. The Miami show on November 25 was a pay-per-view event with special guest appearances from Sheryl Crow, Robert Cray and Bo Diddley. The North American leg of the tour was, again, the highest grossing tour in history at the time. It brought in over $121 million dollars. The closest competition came from Pink Floyd who pulled in more than $103 million dollars on what would be their last tour.

After a break for Christmas and New Years, the tour resumed. This time the Rolling Stones began a five-week run that finally takes them to Mexico, Argentina, Brazil and Chile. These new territories invigorate the Stones with their feverish energy. In Argentina, nearly 400,000 people saw them perform at five shows at River Plate Stadium in Buenos Aires. Immediately following South America, the Rolling Stones made their South

African debut with two shows at Ellis Park in Johannesburg. Nine days later, they returned to Japan for the second time for shows in Tokyo and Fukoka. Then it was on to Australia and New Zealand for their first shows there in 22 years.

The European leg of the tour began with two club shows at the Paradiso Club in Amsterdam. For these shows, which were recorded for a live album, the Stones took a more acoustic approach to much of the set. They also included a number of rarities like "The Spider and the Fly" and "Shine a Light" and some choice covers including the Temptations "I Can't Get Next to You" and Bob Dylan's "Like a Rolling Stone." They performed 37 shows in 16 countries over the summer of 1995. That fall, Stripped, the record cut in Amsterdam with additional tracks recorded in, Lisbon, Paris and Tokyo was released. It was unlike other post-tour releases in that it wasn't merely a document or souvenir from the tour, but a different take on established material. Their version of "Like a Roilling Stone" made it to Number 12 in the U.K.

1996 was a year of well deserved rest. It also saw the long-awaited release of the Rolling Stones Rock and Roll Circus, the Stones' television special filmed in December 1968. Up until this point the only segment that had been legitimately released was the Who's incendiary performance of "A Quick One (While He's Away)" in the documentary The Kids are Alright. In addition to the Who and the Rolling Stones, Jethro Tull (with Tony Iommi of Black Sabbath filling in on guitar), Taj Mahal and one-off super group Dirty Mac (with John Lennon, Keith Richards, Eric Clapton and Mitch Mitchell).

For the first time in their long career, the Rolling Stones set to cut a new record with several different producers helming the sessions. Don Was moved into the title of Executive Producer, along with the Glimmer Twins. He, Danny Saber (U2 and Garbage) and the duo of the Dust Brothers (Beastie Boys, Beck), worked with the Stones in Los Angeles during the spring and early summer of 1997. The four principal members were augmented by a stunning array of supporting talent – Billy Preston, Waddy Wachtel, percussionist Jim Keltner, saxophone legend Wayne Shorter, bassists Me'Shell Ndegeocello and Doug Wimbish – as well as familiar cohorts Darryl Jones, vocalists Bernard Fowler and Blondie Chaplin, and long-serving crew member Pierre De Beauport. This approach led some to speculate that the Stones were conceding to contemporary methods of recording and abandoning their roots. The resulting record, Bridges to Babylon, did employ a different vibe, but to those who paid attention to Voodoo Lounge, this was the next logical step.

Bridges to Babylon dishes out a host of aggressive rock and roll in the songs "Out of Control," "Flip the Switch," "Saint of Me" and "Too Tight." There is an exquisitely dirty edge to "Low Down" and "Might as Well Get Juiced" that make them stand out as not comparable to anything else the Rolling Stones have ever done. Even the mid-tempo numbers and ballads create a completely fresh vibe. Bridges to Babylon reached Number Three in the U.S. and Number Six in the U.K.

The Bridges to Babylon tour was produced by Michael Cohl, as had their previous tours since 1989. This time the Rolling Stones gathered in Toronto, Canada for rehearsals. After two club gigs – one each in Toronto and Chicago – the tour began its September to December run of, mostly stadiums. Taking a cue from U2, the Stones incorporated a smaller satellite stage placed at the opposite end of the stadium where they performed a brief set essentially in the middle of the crowd. The new tour staging was intended to have a bridge that extended over the audience that would carry the group to the smaller stage. Technical problems forced them to abandon the idea and a long runway which bisected the audience was utilized instead. When this first leg of the tour closed, the Stones had grossed nearly $90 million dollars from 36 shows.

1998 started off in a bit of a stutter-step as some shows were cancelled due to a bout of laryngitis suffered by Mick Jagger. He recovered in time for a return to Madison Square Garden. They then move on to Honolulu for their first shows on the island in 25 years. A few west-coast dates and a gig in Mexico are followed by another return to Japan. Whatever troubles Japanese officials had in 1973 are absent as the Stones added Osaka to the itinerary. The 1995 dates in South America proved the viability of the territory and the Rolling Stones returned to Brazil and Argentina, this time co-billing on all shows with Bob Dylan. The previously cancelled U.S. shows were tagged on to the end of this run.

Just a few short weeks before the European tour was to begin, Keith Richards suffered broken ribs when he fell in his library at his home in Connecticut. If that wasn't enough, the World's Greatest Rock and Roll Band had to compete with the biggest sporting event in the world as the World Cup was being hosted in 1998 by France. This led to several cancellations. The tour began in Germany in June and wrapped in Turkey in September. Because of the financial implications of the cancellations and the fact that the band have been working constantly for a year, they decide to make up the dates the following year.

In November, No Security, the third live record of the decade and the seventh overall was released. It contained performances from the U.S., the Netherlands and Argentina. By Rolling Stones standards, it's an eclectic track listing that eschews their biggest hits. It includes five songs from the two most recent studio albums and guest appearances from Taj Mahal, Dave Matthews and Joshua Redman. It reached Number Nine in both the U.S. and the U.K.

Maybe it's because the gargantuan machine that is a Rolling Stones tour is already up and running, 1999 begins with a four-month run of shows in the U.S. The brief European tour only lasts three weeks in May and June. Brevity notwithstanding, it's still the biggest U.S. tour of the year with gross receipts of nearly $65 million dollars.

The next two years are possibly the quietest ever in the Rolling Stones' saga. Band activities ceased but the band members didn't simply sit still. Most active of the group was Charlie Watts. He and Jim Keltner released a record of percussion based tracks each named after a respected jazz drummer. Watts also played live with a few incarnations of his jazz groups. Ron Wood released two solo albums, Live and Eclectic and Not for Beginners. Mick Jagger cut and released his fourth solo outing, Goddess in the Doorway. The closest thing to a Stones performance came when Jagger and Keith Richards appeared together in October 2001 at the Concert for New York City, a benefit show to help the families of public safety workers who perished in the aftermath of the September 11th attacks.

2002 marked 40 years since the group first played under the name the Rolling Stones. To mark the anniversary, Rolling Stones Records and ABKCO collaborated on the first retrospective package to encompass recordings from their entire career. Forty Licks, as the title implied, contained a total of 40 tracks – 36 hits and four new cuts – with a choice of deluxe or standard packaging. The collection was a massive success and reached Number Two in the U.S.

and the UK. Touring behind a greatest hits package was something they hadn't done since 1975. The hook for this jaunt had the Stones playing venues of different sizes in selected cities. Boston, Chicago, New York, Philadelphia and Los Angeles had the band performing in stadiums, arenas and theaters and the set list would vary depending on the intimacy of the venue. Some shows featured set lists that included blocks of songs from particular albums. The first leg of the tour ran from September to November. It grossed nearly $88 million dollars. They were beat out for the biggest grossing tour of 2002 by Paul McCartney who pulled in over $103 million.

In early 2003 the tour resumed with four weeks of U.S. dates including returns to Chicago, New York, Boston, Los Angeles and Las Vegas. Then it was on to Australia, Japan, Singapore and, for the first time, India. Shows for this run in Thailand and China were set but scrubbed. The summer of 2003 didn't have any of the problems the previous European tour encountered. Like the U.S., a few cities were treated to smaller venue shows. Again, the tour spanned the summer opening in June and concluding in October. The Rolling Stones did one North American performance that summer. Toronto had experienced an outbreak of SARS (Severe Acute Respiratory Syndrome) and was placed under a World Health organization warning. The effect on tourism, a major part of Toronto's economy, was disastrous. The Rolling Stones had all but adopted Toronto as a home base as they rehearsed several tours there and felt a need to help. The Stones initiated a massive concert at Downsview Park in Toronto, a former military site, on July 30, 2003, where more than 450,000 people gathered to watch the Stones headline a show which included, Rush, the Guess Who, the Isley Brothers, and many more. The previously cancelled shows in Hong Kong were rescheduled for November. That fall, the Rolling Stones released a book, According to the Rolling Stones, their official oral history / biography.

The following year, 2004, proved to be one of the most trying for the Rolling Stones when it was revealed that Charlie Watts was being treated for cancer. Fortunately he made a full recovery. The band regrouped again with Don Was to hit the studio again.

A Bigger Bang was the first studio release of original material from the Rolling Stones since 1997, the longest-ever period of time between studio albums in their career. Less sprawling than its predecessor, A Bigger Bang is a sharp-elbow of a record, hitting tough and bluesy with tracks like "Rough Justice," "Oh No, Not You Again," "Driving Too Fast" and "Sweet Neo Con," which also contained a rare bit of political commentary. Keith Richards' barroom ballad "This Place is Empty" is one of his most sophisticated performances. Not forsaking their roots, "Back of May Hand" conjures up Muddy Waters on the porch of a Mississippi shack. It is yet another album chart hit achieving Number Two in the U.K. and Number 3 in the U.S.

The Bigger Bang tour brought the Rolling Stones back for another world tour. Starting in Late August, the North American dates ran into February 2006. Then it was on to South America again. In Brazil, the Stones played a free show on Rio de Janeiro's Copacabana Beach to an audience estimated at 1.3 million people. Two more shows in Argentina are followed by two more in Mexico and a brief return to the U.S. March and April take the group back to Japan, Australia and New Zealand. They made their mainland China debut with a concert in Shanghai.

Misfortune struck again when Keith Richards severely injured himself when he fell from a tree while on holiday in Fiji. His surgery and recovery forced several cancellations and pushed the tour into the next year.

The European dates began in July 2006 and ran until early September. Another North American leg began right after and took them through November. Two shows at the Beacon Theatre in New York were filmed by esteemed director Martin Scorsese for a theatrical release. It's Scorsese's first concert film since his highly acclaimed document of the Band's final show, The Last Waltz. The Stones included guest turns from singer Christina Aguilera, Jack White of the White Stripes and blues guitar legend Buddy Guy. The 2005 and 2006 tours are the most lucrative in history and in North America alone gross an astounding $300 million dollars. The make up dates for Europe bloom into another three-month run which wrapped up in London with three nights at the O2 Arena in August 2007.

The Rolling Stones hit the film festival circuit in support of their new picture directed by Martin Scorsese. The group attended the premiers in both Berlin and London in February 2008. The film spawned a soundtrack that was released as a single and double disc. The DVD followed in July. The Stones also signed a new deal with Universal Music Group, the world's largest music company, to bring their catalog to the label.

The back catalog became the focus of most Rolling Stones activities for 2009 and 2010. The 1965 film Charlie is My Darling came out on DVD. Get Yer Ya-Yas Out was re-released as a deluxe four-disc set including previously unreleased tracks and film from the Stones plus sets from B.B. King and Ike and Tina Turner, who opened the New York shows in 1969. Exile on Main Street was reissued in 2010 with a second disc of previously unreleased songs, some of which dated to 1968. Sessions were held to complete some of the unfinished tracks. Jagger, Richards and Mick Taylor all made contributions. A massive roll-out for Exile included a new documentary on the making of the album. Ladies and Gentlemen, The Rolling Stones, the film of the 1972 U.S. tour for Exile was finally released on DVD.

Since the Stones were not touring in 2010, Ron Wood took the opportunity to reunite/reconstitute the Faces. Along with original members Kenny Jones and Ian McLagan, they added Sex Pistols bassist Glen Matlock to fill in for the deceased Ronnie Lane and Simply Red vocalist Mick Hucknall deputized for Rod Stewart who declined to participate.

The final word in reflection and review came when Keith Richards released his long-awaited autobiography, Life. It was very positively reviewed and became an instant bestseller. It also stoked many of the long-simmering issues between him and Mick Jagger.

The story of the Rolling Stones isn't over. Lack of activities like tours or records isn't the litmus test. The Rolling Stones will continue as long as they are of able body and inclination. Keith Richards has always pointed out that his musical heroes played until they dropped. The work ethic of the Rolling Stones should make one expect nothing less.

194 The Rolling Stones photographed in Rome near the end of their epic 2005- 2007 world tour. The U.S. dates alone grossed nearly $300 million dollars.

202-203 Darryl Jones and Mick Jagger kicking off a show on the Voodoo Lounge tour.

204 and 205 Since their first tour of the United States in 1964, New York City has embraced the Rolling Stones. They've performed at virtually every ma- jor venue in the region except for Yan- kee Stadium. Mick Jagger and Keith Richards are seen here performing at Giants Stadium in 1994.

206 and 207 The Rolling Stones meet the media under the Brooklyn Bridge to announce their 1997 Bridges to Babylon tour. The group arrived in a classic American convertible with Jagger at the wheel.

208 and 208-209 The Rolling Stones at the Giants Stadium in New Jersey during the Bridges to Babylon tour, which began on September 9, 1997 in Toronto.

210 Ron Wood seemingly unable to contain himself as Keith Richards holds down the groove behind him.

211 The "principals," Mick Jagger, Ron Wood, Keith Richards and Charlie Watts take a final bow.

212 Keith Richards: in the short list of humans who can pull off wearing a full-length leopard print coat.

213 The Rolling Stones have continually pioneered technically superior and visually stunning concert staging.

214 Ron Wood doesn't let smoking get in the way of whipping off some licks on his Baby Sitar.

215 Wood and Keith Richards locking in together as they practice the ancient art of guitar weaving.

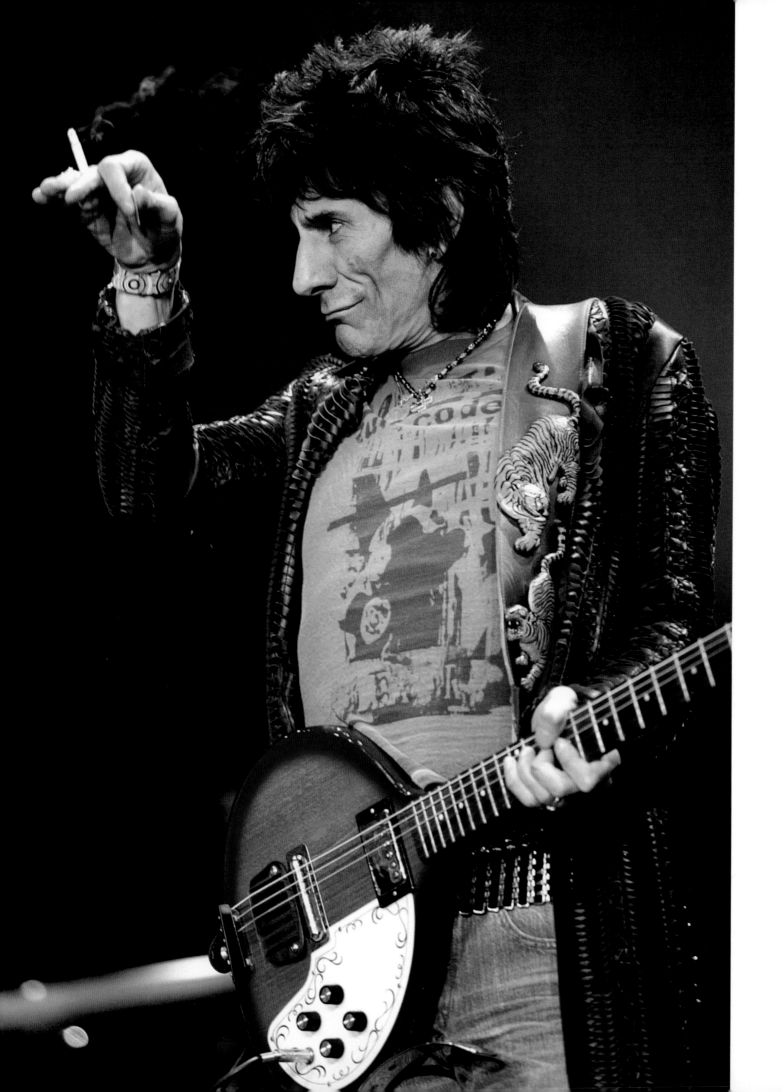

CHARLIE WATTS

"IT DOESN'T REALLY CHANGE, ACTUALLY
I THINK THE ROLLING STONES
HAVE GOTTEN A LOT BETTER
AN AWFUL LOT BETTER I THINK
A LOT OF PEOPLE DON'T
BUT I THINK THEY HAVE
AND TO ME
THAT'S GRATIFYING
IT'S WORTH IT"

licks world tour

217 Ron Wood and Mick Jagger work the edge of the stage as they kick off the 2002 Licks tour in Boston.

218-219 The Rolling Stones at the Fleet Center in Boston, September 3, 2002. It was one of three shows at three different venues in the Boston area.

ROLLINGSTONES

220-221 Mick Jagger getting close with the people as he works the runway in Boston, 2002.

222 and 223 You got to feel it if you're going to play it and Keith Richards feels it from the ground up.

224 and 225 Mick Jagger, the quintessential rock and roll front man, performs at the opening night of the European leg of The Rolling Stones Licks tour at the Olimpiahalle Spiridon in Munich, Germany, June 4, 2003.

226-227 and 227 Mick Jagger is seemingly unable to keep his hands off of Ron Wood during the 2003 Licks tour of Europe.

ROLLING STONES

228 Mick Jagger walks deep into the crowd during a stop on the European leg of the Licks tour in 2003.

228-229 Mick Jagger performs on the European leg of the Licks tour in 2003 at Twickenham Rugby Stadium.

230 and 231 Ronnie Wood and Mick Jagger at the Stade de France in Saint-Denis near Paris. The Rolling Stones played drastically different shows depending upon the size of the venue.

232-233 Mick Jagger, Ronnie Wood, Charlie Watts and Keith Richards during the A Bigger Bang tour, which took place between August 2005 and August 2007 in support of their album A Bigger Bang.

234 and 235 Keith Richards performs

in Amsterdam during the Licks tour.

236-237 and 237 The massive stage for the Licks tour incorporated the latest in large-scale video screen technology.

238-239 The A Bigger Bang tour became the highest grossing concert tour of all time with $558,255,524 earned.

240-241 and 242-243 The A Bigger Bang tour had its official start on 21 August 2005 with two shows at historic Fenway Park in Boston.

244-245 Mick Jagger and Keith Richards during the A Bigger Bang tour. The show included state-of-the-art electronics that presented visual screen shots of the Stones Tongue and live footage.

ROLLINGSTONES

246-247 During the A Bigger Bang tour, as on the Bridges to Babylon and Licks tours, the band played part of the set on a 'B' stage in the center of the field.

248 and 249 Keith Richards and Mick Jagger perform during the Sprint Super Bowl XL halftime show. The game pitted the Seattle Seahawks against the Pittsburgh Steelers at Ford Field in Detroit.

ROLLING
STONES

250 and 250-251 Mick Jagger, Keith Richards and Ronnie Wood during half-time at Super Bowl XL on 5 February 2006 in Detroit.

252 and 253 Mick Jagger and Ronnie Wood performing live onstage during the A Bigger Bang tour.

ROLLINGSTONES

254-255 Mick Jagger on the custom-made lips and tongue-shaped stage in the middle of Ford Field in Detroit when the Rolling Stones performed during the Super Bowl halftime show in 2006.

256 Over one million Rolling Stones fans converge on Copacabana Beach in Rio de Janeiro for a free concert in February 2006.

257 Mick Jagger on stage at the San Siro Stadium in Milan, Italy.

258 and 259 The stage of the A Bigger Bang tour was 25 m (84 ft.) tall. The multilevel construction included balconies behind the stage with accommodations for 400 audience members.

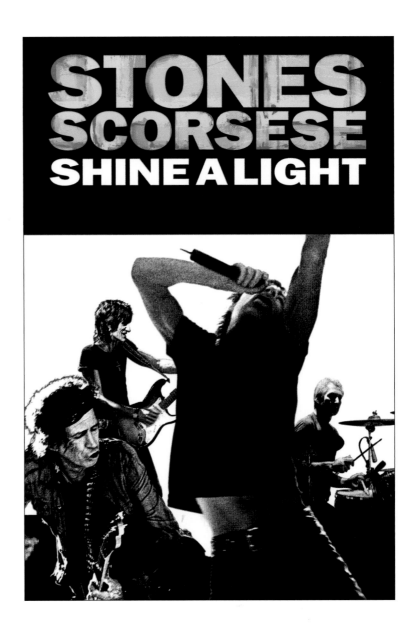

260-261 and 261 The Rolling Stones and legendary film director Martin Scorsese pose at the Beacon Theatre in New York. Scorsese and his team captured two concerts at the intimate venue that became the feature length release Shine a Light. The movie was screened in IMAX as well as standard movie theaters.

263 Mick Jagger at the O2 Arena in London, 23 August 2007.

ROLLINGSTONESROLLINGSTONESROLLINGSTONES
ROLLINGSTONESROLLINGSTONESROLLINGSTONES
ROLLINGSTONESROLLINGSTONESROLLINGSTONES
ROLLINGSTONESROLLINGSTONESROLLINGSTONES
ROLLINGSTONESROLLINGSTONESROLLINGSTONES
ROLLINGSTONESROLLINGSTONESROLLINGSTONES
ROLLINGSTONESROLLINGSTONESROLLINGSTONES
ROLLINGSTONESROLLINGSTONESROLLINGSTONES
ROLLINGSTONESROLLINGSTONESROLLINGSTONES
ROLLINGSTONESROLLINGSTONESROLLINGSTONES
ROLLINGSTONESROLLINGSTONESROLLINGSTONES
ROLLINGSTONESROLLINGSTONESROLLINGSTONES
ROLLINGSTONESROLLINGSTONESROLLINGSTONES
ROLLINGSTONESROLLINGSTONESROLLINGSTONES
ROLLINGSTONESROLLINGSTONESROLLINGSTONES
ROLLINGSTONESROLLINGSTONESROLLINGSTONES
ROLLINGSTONESROLLINGSTONESROLLINGSTONES
ROLLINGSTONESROLLINGSTONESROLLINGSTONES
ROLLINGSTONESROLLINGSTONESROLLINGSTONES
ROLLINGSTONESROLLINGSTONESROLLINGSTONES

 To be continued...

STUDIO ALBUMS

THE ROLLING STONES NO.2 (UK: January 1965)

TRACK LISTING: Everybody Needs Somebody To Love, Down Home Girl, You Can't Catch Me, Time Is On My Side, What A Shame, Grown Up Wrong, Down The Road Apiece, Under The Boardwalk, I Can't Be Satisfied, Pain In My Heart, Off The Hook, Susie Q
LABEL: Decca
PRODUCER: Andrew Loog Oldham
PERSONNEL: Mick Jagger, Brian Jones, Keith Richards, Charlie Watts, Bill Wyman, Ian Stewart (piano, organ), Jack Nitzsche (piano, Nitzsche-phone)

THE ROLLING STONES (UK: April 1964)

Track listing: Route 66, I Just Want To Make Love To You, Honest I Do, Mona (I Need You Baby), Now I've Got A Witness, Little By Little, I'm A King Bee, Carol, Tell Me, Can I Get A Witness, You Can Make It If You Try, Walking The Dog
LABEL: Decca
PRODUCER: Impact Sound
PERSONNEL: Mick Jagger, Brian Jones, Keith Richards, Charlie Watts, Bill Wyman, Ian Stewart (piano, organ), Phil Spector (percussion), Gene Pitney (piano)

THE ROLLING STONES, NOW!
(US: February 1965)

TRACK LISTING: Everybody Needs Somebody to Love, Down Home Girl, You Can't Catch Me, Heart Of Stone, What A Shame, Mona (I Need You Baby), Down The Road Apiece, Off The Hook, Pain In My Heart, Oh Baby (We Got A Good Thing Goin'), Little Red Rooster, Surprise, Surprise
LABEL: London
PRODUCER: Andrew Loog Oldham
PERSONNEL: Mick Jagger, Brian Jones, Keith Richards, Charlie Watts, Bill Wyman, Ian Stewart (piano, organ), Jack Nitzsche (piano, Nitzsche-phone)

ENGLAND'S NEWEST HIT MAKERS
(US: May 1964)

TRACK LISTING: Not Fade Away, Route 66, I Just Want To Make Love To You, Honest I Do, Now I've Got A Witness, Little By Little, I'm A King Bee, Carol, Tell Me, Can I Get A Witness, You Can Make It If You Try, Walking The Dog
LABEL: London
PRODUCER: Impact Sound
PERSONNEL: Mick Jagger, Brian Jones, Keith Richards, Charlie Watts, Bill Wyman, Ian Stewart (piano, organ), Phil Spector (percussion), Gene Pitney (piano)

OUT OF OUR HEADS (US: July 1965)

TRACK LISTING: Mercy, Mercy, Hitch Hike, The Last Time, That's How Strong My Love Is, Good Times, I'm All Right, (I Can't Get No) Satisfaction, Cry To Me, The Under Assistant West Coast Promotion Man, Play With Fire, The Spider And The Fly, One More Try
LABEL: London
PRODUCER: Andrew Loog Oldham
PERSONNEL: Mick Jagger, Brian Jones, Keith Richards, Charlie Watts, Bill Wyman, Ian Stewart (piano, organ), Jack Nitzsche (piano, Nitzsche-phone)

12 X 5 (US: October 1964)

TRACK LISTING: Around & Around, Confessin' The Blues, Empty Heart, Time Is On My Side, Good Times, Bad Times, It's All Over Now, 2120 South Michigan Avenue, Under The Broadwalk, Congratulations, Grown Up Wrong, If You Need Me, Susie-Q
LABEL: London
PRODUCER: Andrew Loog Oldham
PERSONNEL: Mick Jagger, Brian Jones, Keith Richards, Charlie Watts, Bill Wyman

OUT OF OUR HEADS (UK: September 1965)

TRACK LISTING: She Said Yeah, Mercy, Mercy, Hitch Hike, That's How Strong My Love Is, Good Times, Gotta Get Away, Talkin' 'Bout You, Cry To Me, Oh Baby, Heart Of Stone, The Under Assistant West Coast Promotion Man, I'm Free
LABEL: Decca
PRODUCER: Andrew Loog Oldham
PERSONNEL: Mick Jagger, Brian Jones, Keith Richards, Charlie Watts, Bill Wyman, Ian Stewart (piano, organ), Jack Nitzsche (piano, organ, percussion), J.W. Alexander (percussion)

DECEMBER'S CHILDREN (US: December 1965)

TRACK LISTING: She Said Yeah, Talkin' About You, You Better Move On, Look What You've Done, The Singer Not The Song, Route 66, Get Off Of My Cloud, I'm Free, As Tears Go By, Gotta Get Away, Blue Turns To Grey, I'm Moving On, Route 66 (live)
LABEL: London
PRODUCER: Andrew Loog Oldham
PERSONNEL: Mick Jagger, Brian Jones, Keith Richards, Charlie Watts, Bill Wyman

BETWEEN THE BUTTONS (US: February 1967)

TRACK LISTING: Let's Spend The Night Together, Yesterday's Papers, Ruby Tuesday, Connection, She Smiled Sweetly, Cool Calm And Collected, All Sold Out, My Obsession, Who's Been Sleeping Here, Complicated, Miss Amanda Jones, Something Happened To Me Yesterday
LABEL: London
PRODUCER: Andrew Loog Oldham
PERSONNEL: Mick Jagger, Brian Jones, Keith Richards, Charlie Watts, Bill Wyman

AFTERMATH (UK: April 1966)

TRACK LISTING: Mother's Little Helper, Stupid Girl, Lady Jane, Under My Thumb, Doncha Bother Me, Goin' Home, Flight 505, High And Dry, Out Of Time, It's Not Easy, I Am Waiting, Take It Or Leave It, Think, What To Do
LABEL: Decca
PRODUCER: Andrew Loog Oldham
PERSONNEL: Mick Jagger, Brian Jones, Keith Richards, Charlie Watts, Bill Wyman, Ian Stewart (piano, percussion), Jack Nitzsche (piano, organ, percussion)

THEIR SATANIC MAJESTIES REQUEST (UK-US: December-November 1967)

TRACK LISTING: Sing This All Together, Citadel, In Another Land, 2000 Man, Sing This All Together (See What Happens), She's A Rainbow, The Lantern, Gomper, 2000 Light Years From Home, On With The Show
LABEL: Decca/London
PRODUCER: The Rolling Stones
PERSONNEL: Mick Jagger, Brian Jones, Keith Richards, Charlie Watts, Bill Wyman

AFTERMATH (US: July 1966)

TRACK LISTING: Paint It Black, Stupid Girl, Lady Jane, Under My Thumb, Doncha Bother Me, Think, Flight 505, High And Dry, It's Not Easy, I Am Waiting, Going Home
LABEL: London
PRODUCER: Andrew Loog Oldham
PERSONNEL: Mick Jagger, Brian Jones, Keith Richards, Charlie Watts, Bill Wyman, Ian Stewart (piano, percussion), Jack Nitzsche (piano, organ, percussion)

BEGGARS BANQUET (UK-US: December-November 1968)

TRACK LISTING: Sympathy For The Devil, No Expectations, Dear Doctor, Parachute Woman, Jigsaw Puzzle, Street Fighting Man, Prodigal Son, Stray Cat Blues, Factory Girl, Salt Of The Earth
LABEL: Decca/London
PRODUCER: Jimmy Miller
PERSONNEL: Mick Jagger, Brian Jones, Keith Richards, Charlie Watts, Bill Wyman, Nicky Hopkins (piano)

BETWEEN THE BUTTONS (UK: January 1967)

TRACK LISTING: Let's Spend The Night Together, Yesterday's Papers, Ruby Tuesday, Connection, She Smiled Sweetly, Cool Calm And Collected, All Sold Out, My Obsession, Who's Been Sleeping Here, Complicated, Miss Amanda Jones, Something Happened To Me Yesterday
LABEL: Decca
PRODUCER: Andrew Loog Oldham
PERSONNEL: Mick Jagger, Brian Jones, Keith Richards, Charlie Watts, Bill Wyman

LET IT BLEED (UK-US: December-November 1969)

TRACK LISTING: Gimme Shelter, Love In Vain, Country Honk, Live With Me, Let It Bleed, Midnight Rambler, You Got The Silver, Monkey Man, You Can't Always Get What You Want
LABEL: Decca/London
PRODUCER: Jimmy Miller
PERSONNEL: Mick Jagger, Keith Richards, Mick Taylor, Charlie Watts, Bill Wyman, Merry Clayton, Madeline Bell, Doris Troy, Nanette Newman (vocals), Nicky Hopkins (piano, organ), Jimmy Miller (drums, percussion), Al Kooper (piano, French horn), Byron Berline (fiddle), Ry Cooder (mandolin), Leon Russell (piano), Ian Stewart (piano), Bobby Keys (sax), Rocky Dijon (percussion), The London Bach Choir (vocals)

STICKY FINGERS (UK-US: April-June 1971)

TRACK LISTING: Brown Sugar, Sway, Wild Horses, Can't You Hear Me Knocking, You Gotta Move, Bitch, I Got The Blues, Sister Morphine, Dead Flowers, Moonlight Mile
LABEL: Rolling Stones
PRODUCER: Jimmy Miller
PERSONNEL: Mick Jagger, Keith Richards, Mick Taylor, Charlie Watts, Bill Wyman, Nicky Hopkins (piano, organ), Jimmy Miller (percussion), Ry Cooder (guitar), Jimmy Dickinson (piano), Ian Stewart (piano), Bobby Keys (sax), Rocky Dijon (percussion), Jim Price (trumpet, piano), Jack Nitzsche (piano)

EXILE ON MAIN STREET (UK-US: May 1972)

TRACK LISTING: Rocks Off, Rip This Joint, Shake Your Hips, Casino Boogie, Tumbling Dice, Sweet Virginia, Torn And Frayed, Sweet Black Angel, Loving Cup, Happy, Turd On The Run, Ventilator Blues, I Just Want To See His Face, Let It Loose, All Down The Line, Stop Breaking Down, Shine A Light, Soul Survivor
LABEL: Rolling Stones
PRODUCER: Jimmy Miller
PERSONNEL: Mick Jagger, Keith Richards, Mick Taylor, Charlie Watts, Bill Wyman, Bill Plummer (upright bass), Ian Stewart (piano), Nicky Hopkins (piano), Clydie King, Vanetta Fields, Tammi Lynn, Kathy McDonald, Shirley Goodman (vocals), Mac Rebennack (vocals), Joe Green (vocals), Al Perkins (steel guitar), Jim Price (trumpet, trombone, piano), Jimmy Miller (percussion), Bobby Keys (sax), Billy Preston (organ), Jerry Kirkle (vocals)

GOATS HEAD SOUP (UK-US: August 1973)

TRACK LISTING: Dancing With Mr D., 100 Years Ago, Coming Down Again, Doo Doo Doo Doo Doo (Heartbreaker), Angie, Silver Train, Hide Your Love, Winter, Can You Hear The Music, Star Star
LABEL: Rolling Stones
PRODUCER: Jimmy Miller
PERSONNEL: Mick Jagger, Keith Richards, Mick Taylor, Charlie Watts, Bill Wyman, Nicky Hopkins (piano), Billy Preston (piano, clavinet), Ian Stewart (piano, jangles), Bobby Keys (sax), Jim Horn (sax, flute), Chuck Finley (trumpet), Jim Price (horns), Jimmy Miller, Pascal, Reebop (percussion)

IT'S ONLY ROCK N' ROLL (UK-US: October 1974)

TRACK LISTING: If You Can't Rock Me, Ain't Too Proud To Beg, It's Only Rock 'n Roll (But I Like It), Till The Next Goodbye, Time Waits For No One, Luxury, Dance Little Sister, If You Really Want To Be My Friend, Short And Curlies, Fingerprint File
LABEL: Rolling Stones
PRODUCER: The Glimmer Twins (Jagger-Richards)
PERSONNEL: Mick Jagger, Keith Richards, Mick Taylor, Charlie Watts, Bill Wyman, Willie Weeks (bass guitar), Kenney Jones (drums), Billy Preston (piano, clavinet), Nicky Hopkins (piano), Charlie Jolly (tabla), Ray Cooper (percussion), Blue Magic (vocals)

BLACK AND BLUE (UK-US: April 1976)

TRACK LISTING: Hot Stuff, Hand Of Fate, Cherry Oh Baby, Memory Motel, Hey Negrita, Melody, Fool To Cry, Crazy Mama
LABEL: Rolling Stones
PRODUCER: The Glimmer Twins
PERSONNEL: Mick Jagger, Keith Richards, Charlie Watts, Ron Wood, Bill Wyman, Harvey Mandel (guitar), Wayne Perkins (guitar), Billy Preston (piano, organ, synthesiser), Ollie E. Brown (percussion), Nicky Hopkins (piano, organ)

SOME GIRLS (UK-US: June 1978)

TRACK LISTING: Miss You, When The Whip Comes Down, Just My Imagination (Running Away With Me), Some Girls, Lies, Far Away Eyes, Respectable, Before They Make Me Run, Beast Of Burden, Shattered
LABEL: Rolling Stones
PRODUCER: The Glimmer Twins
PERSONNEL: Mick Jagger, Keith Richards, Charlie Watts, Ron Wood, Bill Wyman, Ian McLagan (piano, organ), Mel Collins (sax), Sugar Blue (harmonica)

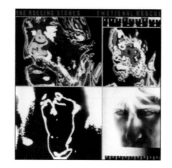

EMOTIONAL RESCUE (UK-US: June 1980)

TRACK LISTING: Dance, Summer Romance, Send It To Me, Let Me Go, Indian Girl, Where The Boys Go, Down In The Hole, Emotional Rescue, She's So Cold, All About You
LABEL: Rolling Stones
PRODUCER: The Glimmer Twins
PERSONNEL: Mick Jagger, Keith Richards, Charlie Watts, Ron Wood, Bill Wyman, Ian Stewart (piano), Bobby Keys (sax), Sugar Blue (harmonica), Michael Shrieve (percussion), Max Romeo (vocals)

TATTOO YOU (UK-US: August 1981)

TRACK LISTING: Start Me Up, Hang Fire, Slave, Little T&A, Black Limousine, Neighbors, Worried About You, Tops, Heaven, No Use In Crying, Waiting On A Friend
LABEL: Rolling Stones
PRODUCER: The Glimmer Twins
PERSONNEL: Mick Jagger, Keith Richards, Charlie Watts, Ron Wood, Bill Wyman, Sonny Rollins (sax), Ian Stewart (piano), Billy Preston (keyboards), Nicky Hopkins (keyboards), Wayne Perkins (guitar), Jeff Beck (guitar), Pete Townshend (guitar)

UNDERCOVER (US-UK: November 1983)

TRACK LISTING: Undercover Of The Night, She Was Hot, Tie You Up (The Pain Of Love), Wanna Hold You, Feel On Baby, Too Much Blood, Pretty Beat, Up, Too Tough, All The Way Down, It Must Be Hell
LABEL: Rolling Stones
PRODUCER: The Glimmer Twins and Chris Kimsey
PERSONNEL: Mick Jagger, Keith Richards, Charlie Watts, Ron Wood, Bill Wyman, Moustapha Cisse, Brahms Coundoul, Martin Ditcham, Sly Dunbar (percussion), Ian Stewart (piano), David Sanborn (sax), Chuck Leavell (keyboards), Jim Barber (guitar), CHOPS (horns)

DIRTY WORK (UK-US: March 1986)

TRACK LISTING: One Hit (To The Body), Fight, Harlem Shuffle, Hold Back, Too Rude, Winning Ugly, Back To Zero, Dirty Work, Had It With You, Sleep Tonight, Key To The Highway
LABEL: Rolling Stones
PRODUCER: The Glimmer Twins and Steve Lillywhite
PERSONNEL: Mick Jagger, Keith Richards, Charlie Watts, Ron Wood, Bill Wyman, Chuck Leavell (keyboards), Jimmy Page (guitar), Kirsty MacColl, Beverly D'Angelo, Bobby Womack, Jimmy Cliff, Tom Waits, Don Covay, Patti Scialfa, Janice Pendarvis, Dollette McDonald (vocals), Ivan Neville (keyboards, bass guitar), Anton Fig (percussion), Dan Collette (trumpet), Chuck Leavell (keyboards), Ian Stewart (piano)

STEEL WHEELS (US-UK: August-September 1989)

TRACK LISTING: Sad Sad Sad, Mixed Emotions, Terrifying, Hold On To Your Hat, Hearts For Sale, Blinded By Love, Rock And A Hard Place, Can't Be Seen, Almost Hear You Sigh, Continental Drift, Break The Spell, Slipping Away
LABEL: Rolling Stones
PRODUCER: The Glimmer Twins and Chris Kimsey
PERSONNEL: Mick Jagger, Keith Richards, Charlie Watts, Ron Wood, Bill Wyman, Chuck Leavell (piano, organ), Kick Horns, Bernard Fowler, Sarah Dash, Lisa Fischer (vocals), Luis Jardim (percussion), Matt Clifford (keyboards), Phil Beer (fiddle, mandolin), Roddy Lorimer (trumpet), The Master Musicians of Joujouka

VOODOO LOUNGE (UK-US: July 1994)

TRACK LISTING: Love Is Strong, You Got Me Rocking, Sparks Will Fly, The Worst, New Faces, Moon Is Up, Out Of Tears, I Go Wild, Brand New Car, Sweethearts Together, Suck On The Jugular, Blinded By Rainbows, Baby Break It Down, Thru And Thru, Mean Disposition
LABEL: Rolling Stones
PRODUCER: Don Was and The Glimmer Twins
PERSONNEL: Mick Jagger, Keith Richards, Charlie Watts, Ron Wood, Darryl Jones (bass guitar), Chuck Leavell (keyboards), Bernard Fowler (vocals), Ivan Neville (organ), David McMurray (sax), Mark Isham (trumpet), Lenny Castro (percussion), Luis Jardim (percussion), Bobby Womack (vocals), Frankie Gavin (fiddle), Pierre de Beauport (guitar), Flaco Jimenez (accordion), Max Baca (bajo sexto), Phil Jones (percussion)

BRIDGES TO BABYLON (UK-US: September 1997)

TRACK LISTING: Flip The Switch, Anybody Seen My Baby, Low Down, Already Over Me, Gunface, You Don't Have To Mean It, Out Of Control, Saint Of Me, Might As Well Get Juiced, Always Suffering, Too Tight, Thief In The Night, How Can I Stop
LABEL: Rolling Stones
PRODUCER: Don Was and The Glimmer Twins
PERSONNEL: Mick Jagger, Keith Richards, Charlie Watts, Ron Wood, Darryl Jones (bass guitar), Waddy Wachtel (guitar), Benmont Tench (keyboards), Doug Wimbish (bass guitar), Jim Keltner (percussion), Darrell Leonard, Joe Sublett, Wayne Shorter (sax), Bernard Fowler (vocals), Clinton Clifford, Danny Saber (keyboards), Blondie Chaplin (vocals, piano), Jeff Sarli (bass guitar), Jamie Muhoberac (bass guitar, keyboards), Don Was (keyboards), Pierre de Beauport (keyboards, bass guitar), Me'Shell Ndegeocello (bass guitar)

A BIGGER BANG (UK-US: September 2005)

TRACK LISTING: Rough Justice, Let Me Down Slow, It Won't Take Long, Rain Fall Down, Streets Of Love, Back Of My Hand, She Saw Me Coming, Biggest Mistake, This Place Is Empty, Oh No, Not You Again, Dangerous Beauty, Laugh, I Nearly Died, Sweet Neo Con, Look What The Cat Dragged In, Driving Too Fast, Infamy
LABEL: Virgin, Interscope, Polydor
PRODUCER: Don Was and The Glimmer Twins
PERSONNEL: Mick Jagger, Keith Richards, Charlie Watts, Ron Wood, Darryl Jones (bass guitar), Lenny Castro (percussion), Blondie Chaplin (vocals), Matt Clifford (keyboards), Chuck Leavell (keyboards), Don Was (piano)

SELECTED LIVE ALBUMS

GET YER YA-YA'S OUT! (UK-US: September 1969)

TRACK LISTING: Jumpin' Jack Flash, Carol, Stray Cat Blues, Love In Vain, Midnight Rambler, Sympathy For The Devil, Live With Me, Little Queenie, Honky Tonk Women, Street Fighting Man

LABEL: Decca/London

PRODUCER: The Rolling Stones and Glyn Johns

PERSONNEL: Mick Jagger, Keith Richards, Mick Taylor, Charlie Watts, Bill Wyman, Ian Stewart (piano)

STRIPPED (UK-US: November 1995)

TRACK LISTING: Street Fighting Man, Like A Rolling Stone, Not Fade Away, Shine A Light, The Spider And The Fly, I'm Free, Wild Horses, Let It Bleed, Dead Flowers, Slipping Away, Angie, Love In Vain, Sweet Virginia, Little Baby

LABEL: Rolling Stones

PRODUCER: The Glimmer Twins and Don Was

PERSONNEL: Mick Jagger, Keith Richards, Charlie Watts, Ron Wood, Darryl Jones (bass guitar), Chuck Leavell (keyboards), Bernard Fowler (vocals), Lisa Fischer (vocals), Bobby Keys (sax), Andy Snitzer (sax), Michael Davis (trombone), Kent Smith (trumpet)

LOVE YOU LIVE (US-UK: September 1976)

TRACK LISTING: Fanfare For The Common Man, Honky Tonk Woman, If You Can't Rock Me-Get Off My Cloud, Happy, Hot Stuff, Star Star, Tumbling Dice, Fingerprint File, You Gotta Move, You Can't Always Get What You Want, Mannish Boy, Crackin' Up, Little Red Rooster, Around And Around, It's Only Rock N' Roll, Brown Sugar, Jumpin' Jack Flash, Sympathy For The Devil

LABEL: Rolling Stones

PRODUCER: The Glimmer Twins

PERSONNEL: Mick Jagger, Keith Richards, Charlie Watts, Ron Wood, Bill Wyman, Billy Preston (keyboards, vocals), Ian Stewart (piano), Ollie Brown (percussion)

SHINE A LIGHT (UK-US: April 2008)

TRACK LISTING: Jumpin' Jack Flash, Shattered, She Was Hot, All Down The Line, Loving Cup (With Jack White), As Tears Go By, Some Girls, Just My Imagination, Faraway Eyes, Champagne And Reefer (With Buddy Guy), Tumbling Dice, Band Introductions, You Got The Silver, Connection, Martin Scorsese Intro, Sympathy For The Devil, Live With Me (With Christina Aguilera), Start Me Up, Brown Sugar, (I Can't Get No) Satisfaction, Paint It Black, Little T&A, I'm Free, Shine A Light

LABEL: Polydor

PRODUCER: The Glimmer Twins and Bob Clearmountain

PERSONNEL: Mick Jagger, Keith Richards, Charlie Watts, Ron Wood, Darryl Jones (bass guitar), Christina Aguilera (vocals), Buddy Guy (guitar, vocals), Jack White (guitar, vocals), Chuck Leavell (keyboards), Lisa Fischer, Bernard Fowler (vocals), Blondie Chaplin (guitar, vocals), Bobby Keys (sax), Michael Davis (trombone), Kent Smith (trumpet), Tim Ries (sax, keyboards)

OTHER LIVE ALBUMS

Got Live If You Want It!, 1966 (US only)
Still Life (American Concert 1981), 1982
Flashpoint, 1991
No Security, 1998
Live Licks, 2004

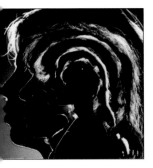

HOT ROCKS 1964-1971
(US: January 1971 - reissued 1990)

TRACK LISTING: Time Is On My Side, Heart Of Stone, Play With Fire, (I Can't Get No) Satisfaction, As Tears Go By, Get Off Of My Cloud, Mother's Little Helper, 19th Nervous Breakdown, Paint It Black, Under My Thumb, Ruby Tuesday, Let's Spend The Night Together, Jumping Jack Flash, Street Fighting Man, Sympathy For The Devil, Honky Tonk Women, Gimme Shelter, Midnight Rambler (Live), You Can't Always Get What You Want, Brown Sugar, Wild Horses

LABEL: London

PRODUCER: Andrew Loog Oldham and Jimmy Miller

PERSONNEL: Mick Jagger, Keith Richards, Mick Taylor, Charlie Watts, Bill Wyman, various others

JUMP BACK
THE BEST OF THE ROLLING STONES 1971- 1993
(UK: November 1993, US: August 2004)

TRACK LISTING: Start Me Up, Brown Sugar, Harlem Shuffle, It's Only Rock N' Roll, Mixed Emotions, Angie, Tumbling Dice, Fool To Cry, Rock And A Hard Place, Miss You, Hot Stuff, Emotional Rescue, Respectable, Beast Of Burden, Waiting On A Friend, Wild Horses, Bitch, Undercover Of The Night

LABEL: Rolling Stones

PRODUCER: various

PERSONNEL: Mick Jagger, Keith Richards, Mick Taylor, Charlie Watts, Ron Wood, Bill Wyman, various others

SUCKING IN THE SEVENTIES
(UK-US: March-April 1981)

TRACK LISTING: Shattered (Live 1981), Everything Is Turning To Gold, Hot Stuff, Time Waits For No One, Fool To Cry, Mannish Boy, When The Whip Comes Down (Live), If I Was A Dancer (Dance Pt. 2), Crazy Mama, Beast Of Burden

LABEL: Rolling Stones

PRODUCER: The Glimmer Twins

PERSONNEL: Mick Jagger, Keith Richards, Mick Taylor, Charlie Watts, Ron Wood, Bill Wyman

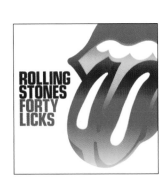

FORTY LICKS (UK-US: October 2002)

TRACK LISTING: Street Fighting Man, Gimme Shelter, (I Can't Get No) Satisfaction, The Last Time, Jumpin' Jack Flash, You Can't Always Get What You Want, 19th Nervous Breakdown, Under My Thumb, Not Fade Away, Have You Seen Your Mother, Baby, Standing In The Shadow, Sympathy For The Devil, Mother's Little Helper, She's A Rainbow, Get Off Of My Cloud, Wild Horses, Ruby Tuesday, Paint It Black, Honky Tonk Women, It's All Over Now, Let's Spend The Night Together, Start Me Up, Brown Sugar, Miss You, Beast Of Burden, Don't Stop, Happy, Angie, You Got Me Rocking, Shattered, Fool To Cry, Love Is Strong, Mixed Emotions, Keys To Your Love, Anybody Seen My Baby, Stealing My Heart, Tumbling Dice, Undercover Of The Night, Emotional Rescue, It's Only Rock N' Roll, Losing My Touch

LABEL: Rolling Stones

PRODUCER: various

PERSONNEL: Mick Jagger, Brian Jones, Keith Richards, Mick Taylor, Charlie Watts, Ron Wood, Bill Wyman, various others

SINGLES COLLECTION THE LONDON YEARS
(US: August 1989)

TRACK LISTING: Come On, I Want To Be Loved, I Wanna Be Your Man, Stoned, Not Fade Away, Little By Little, It's All Over Now, Good Times, Bad Times, Tell Me, I Just Want To Make Love To You, Time Is On My Side, Congratulations, Little Red Rooster, Off The Hook, Heart Of Stone, What a Shame, The Last Time, Play With Fire, (I Can't Get No) Satisfaction, The Under Assistant West Coast Promotion Man, The Spider And The Fly, Get Off Of My Cloud, I'm Free, The Singer Not The Song, As Tears Go By, Gotta Get Away, 19th Nervous Breakdown, Sad Day, Paint It Black, Stupid Girl, Long, Long While, Mother's Little Helper, Lady Jane, Have You Seen Your Mother, Baby, Standing In The Shadow, Who's Driving Your Plane, Let's Spend The Night Together, Ruby Tuesday, We Love You, Dandelion, She's A Rainbow, 2000 Light Years From Home, In Another Land, The Lantern, Jumpin' Jack Flash, Child Of The Moon, Street Fighting Man, No Expectations, Surprise, Surpise, Honky Tonk Women, You Can't Always Get What You Want, Memo From Turner, Brown Sugar, Wild Horses, I Don't Know Whay AKA Don't Know Why I Love You, Try A Little Harder, Out Of Time, Jiving Sister Fanny, Sympathy For The Devil

LABEL: ABKCO

PRODUCER: Andrew Loog Oldham and Jimmy Miller

PERSONNEL: Mick Jagger, Brian Jones, Keith Richards, Mick Taylor, Charlie Watts, Bill Wyman, various others

OTHER COMPILATIONS

Big Hits (High Tides and Green Grass), 1966
Through the Past, Darkly (Big Hits Vol. 2), 1969
More Hot Rocks (Big Hits and Fazed Cookies), 1972
Made in the Shade, 1975
Time Waits For No One, 1979
Rewind (1971-1984), 1984
Rarities (1971-2003), 2005
The Rolling Stones Singles (1971-2006), 2011

SELECTED
COMPILATIONS

BIBLIOGRAPHY

According to the Rolling Stones, Mick Jagger, Keith Richards, Charlie Watts, Ronnie Wood (Chronicle, 2003)

Atlantic/Atco Bulletin 'Stones Tour 78' edition, September 11, 1978

It's Only Rock and Roll: The Ultimate Guide to the Rolling Stones by James Karnbach and Carol Bernson (Facts on File, 1997)

Life, Keith Richards with James Fox, (Little Brown, 2010)

NME Originals: The Rolling Stones (IPC Ignite, Volume 1, issue 9, 2003)

Pollstar Magazine, January 17, 2011

The Rolling Stones: An Illustrated Record, Roy Carr (Harmony, 1976)

The Rolling Stones Chronicle, Massimo Bonanno (Plexus, 1990)

The Rolling Stones: Complete Recording Sessions, Martin Elliott (Blandford, 1990)

Rolling With the Stones, Bill Wyman (Dorling Kindersley, 2002)

PHOTO CREDITS

Pages 2/3 Picture Alliance/Photoshot

Page 4 Michael Ochs Archives/Stringer/Getty Images

Page 6 KMazur/WiewImage/Getty

Page 10 A. Messerschmidt/Getty Images

Page 11 Terry O'Neil/Getty Images

Page 12 Michael Ochs Archives/Stringer/Getty Images

Page 13 Terry O'Neil/Getty Images

Pages 14 Hulton Archive/Getty Images

Pages 15 Lichfield Archive/Getty Images

Page 16 Express Newspapers/Hulton Archive/Getty Images

Page 21 Michael Ochs Archives/Stringer/Getty Images

Pages 26/27 Pierre Fournier/Sygma/Corbis

Pages 28/29 Fiona Adams/Redferns/Getty Images

Pages 30/31 Terry O'Neil/Getty Images

Pages 32/33 Mark and Colleen Hayward/Hulton Archive/Getty Images

Page 34 Peter Francis/Redferns/Getty Images

Page 35 Peter Francis/Redferns/Getty Images

Pages 36/37 Terry O'Neil/Getty Images

Page 37 Terry O'Neil/Getty Images

Pages 38/39 Terry O'Neil/Getty Images

Page 39 Terry O'Neil/Getty Images

Page 40 Pierre Fournier/Sygma/Corbis

Pages 42/43 William Lovelace/Hulton Archive/Getty Images

Page 43 William Lovelace/Hulton Archive/Getty Images

Page 44 Terry O'Neil/Getty Images

Pages 44/45 Terry O'Neil/Getty Images

Page 46 Terry O'Neil/Getty Images

Pages 46/47 Terry O'Neil/Getty Images

Page 48 Jan Persson/Redferns/Getty Images

Page 49 Davies/Hulton Archive/Getty Images

Pages 50/51 David Redferns/Getty Images

Page 52 David Redferns/Getty Images

Page 53 David Redferns/Getty Images

Pages 54/55 Mirrorpix

Page 56 Ted West/Hulton Archive/Getty Images

Page 57 Stanley Sherman/Hulton Archive/Getty Images

Pages 58/59 Michael Ochs Archives/Getty Images

Page 60 John Reader/ Time & Life Images/Getty Images

Page 61 John Reader/ Time & Life Images/Getty Images

Pages 62/63 Mirrorpix

Pages 64/65 Larry Ellis/Hulton Archives/Getty Images

Pages 66/67 Larry Ellis/Hulton Archives/Getty Images

Page 68 Keystone Features/Hulton Archive/Getty Images

Page 69 Keystone Features/Hulton Archive/Getty Images

Page 70/71 Ivan Keeman/Redferns/Getty Images

Page 72 Robert Knight Archive/Redferns/Getty Images

Pages 80/81 Lichfield Archive//Getty Images

Page 85 Michael Ochs Archives/Getty Images

Page 86 Michael Ochs Archives/Getty Images

Pages 88/89 Eric Piper/Mirrorpix

Page 89 Michael Webb/Hulton Archive/Getty Images

ROLLING**STONES**

Krause Publications, a division of F+W Media, Inc.
700 East State Street • Iola, WI 54990-0001
715-445-2214 • 888-457-2873
www.krausebooks.com

David & Charles is an imprint of F&W Media International, LTD
Brunel House, Forde Close, Newton Abbot, TQ12 4PU, UK

Krause Publications and F&W Media International are
divisions of F+W Media, 4700 East Galbraith Road,
Cincinnati OH45236, USA

© 2011 White Star Publishers,
Via Candido Sassone, 24
13100 Vercelli, Italia
www.whitestar.it

First published 2011

ISBN-13: 978-1-4402-1829-3
ISBN-10: 1-4402-1829-3

A catalogue record for this book is available from the
British Library.

Printed in Indonesia

10 9 8 7 6 5 4 3 2 1